SOUTH SHIELDS TROLLEYBUSES

Stephen Lockwood

Edited by Robert J Harley

MP Middleton Press

Front cover
It was 41 years after the closure of the system before a South Shields trolleybus carried passengers again. Karrier E4 204, newly restored to its original 1937 condition, makes its debut at the Sandtoft Trolleybus Museum in May 2005. (CW Routh)

Rear Cover
This typical scene at Stanhope Road shows a former St Helens trolleybus, 203, turning into Boldon Lane to travel towards Tyne Dock. In the background is another trolleybus of the same type showing the 'Shop at Binns' advertisement which was applied to the rear of all the vehicles. (Author's collection)

> **The trolleybuses in this County Durham town operated a complex network of routes serving such diverse locations as docks, housing estates and the seaside. Through these pages, take a trolley ride around each route in turn, seeing how South Shields looked in the middle of the last century.**

Published August 2007

ISBN 978 1 906008 11 6

© *Middleton Press, 2007*

Design Deborah Esher

Published by
    Middleton Press
    Easebourne Lane
    Midhurst
    West Sussex
    GU29 9AZ
Tel: 01730 813169
Fax: 01730 812601
Email: info@middletonpress.co.uk
www.middletonpress.co.uk

Printed & bound by Biddles Ltd, Kings Lynn

CONTENTS

1	The Last Trams	72	Prince Edward Road and Horsley Hill
3	The First Trolleybuses	76	Marsden: Inn, Bay and Grotto
5	Pier Head and Ocean Road	84	Coast Road and South Beach
11	Fowler Street and Westoe Road	91	The Lawe
18	Westoe	95	Depots
24	Chichester	99	Rolling Stock
29	Stanhope Road	112	On Loan
36	Tyne Dock	113	On Show
42	Laygate and Western Approach	115	On its Side
49	Commercial Road	116	Finale
54	Market Place and King Street	118	Postscript
67	King George Road and The Ridgeway		

INTRODUCTION AND ACKNOWLEDGEMENTS

The trolleybus system at South Shields was one of three to operate in County Durham, and the last of these to survive. Although it was, perhaps, overshadowed in fleet size and extent by its near neighbour Newcastle, the compact South Shields system did have considerable points of interest. This was the trolleybus system which was still running some vehicles with wooden seats in the 1960s, and which changed one route permanently to motorbus operation following a snowstorm. The routes operated reflected the town's dual role as a busy commercial port and also a seaside resort with beaches and cliffs. Having begun operations in the 1930s with a modern fleet, enemy action during the Second World War resulted in the hasty acquisition of a motley collection of cast-offs from other trolleybus towns. In the later stages of the system's life, it seemed to operate in a rather down-at-heel fashion, as described later in this album.

This volume is meant to give a flavour of what the system was like and to give the reader a pictorial tour of the routes operated. It is not intended as a comprehensive history, although by its nature, much historical information is provided. The main work on the subject, *The Trolleybuses of South Shields* by Geoff Burrows, was published in 1976.

For this volume, I have to thank the various people that have assisted me in its compilation, not least the photographers and suppliers of photographs, each of whom is credited individually, where known, in each caption. Special thanks need to be extended to Stanley King, who visited and recorded the system on several occasions, and to Roger Harrison, a friend and work colleague as well as being a 'Shieldsman'. Both these gentlemen have read through my text and offered help and advice accordingly, generally going out of their way to share knowledge with me. Roger has devoted considerable time to undertake local investigations, confirming key dates, and identifying locations shown on some of the photographs, to the extent of resolving matters by driving around the town and comparing past and present roof-lines!

I am grateful to Anne Sharp of South Tyneside Libraries Local Studies Section for her assistance in locating and making available several photographs held in its collection.

Thanks go to Roger Smith, who has produced the excellent overhead wiring maps from my rough drawings: to Terry Russell, who has drawn the scale vehicle diagrams specially prepared for this book: to Eric Old for supplying examples of tickets, and to William Peel of South Sheilds who made available a copy of the Transport Department's Jubilee brochure of 1956 which proved very useful for background information.

Finally, I need to express my appreciation to my wife Eileen, who puts up with all the distractions that are a consequence of preparing a book such as this.

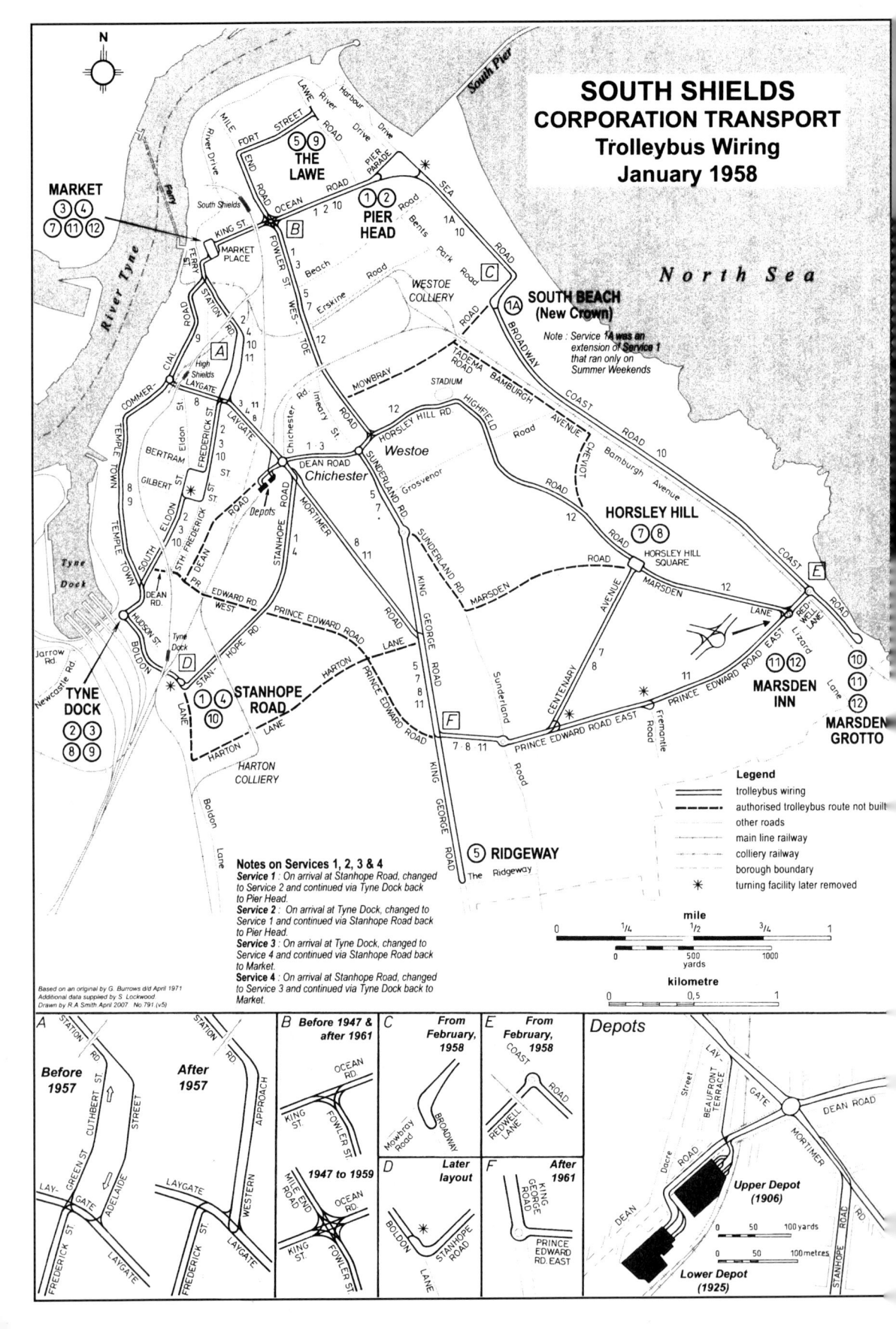

SOUTH SHIELDS CORPORATION TRANSPORT
Trolleybus Wiring
January 1958

MARKET ③ ④ ⑦ ⑪ ⑫

THE LAWE ⑤ ⑨

PIER HEAD ① ②

SOUTH BEACH (New Crown) ①A

Note: Service 1A was an extension of Service 1 that ran only on Summer Weekends

North Sea

HORSLEY HILL ⑦ ⑧

TYNE DOCK ② ③ ⑧ ⑨

STANHOPE ROAD ① ④ ⑩

MARSDEN INN ⑪ ⑫

MARSDEN GROTTO ⑩ ⑪ ⑫

RIDGEWAY ⑤

Legend
- trolleybus wiring
- authorised trolleybus route not built
- other roads
- main line railway
- colliery railway
- borough boundary
- ✳ turning facility later removed

Notes on Services 1, 2, 3 & 4
Service 1: On arrival at Stanhope Road, changed to Service 2 and continued via Tyne Dock back to Pier Head.
Service 2: On arrival at Tyne Dock, changed to Service 1 and continued via Stanhope Road back to Pier Head.
Service 3: On arrival at Tyne Dock, changed to Service 4 and continued via Stanhope Road back to Market.
Service 4: On arrival at Stanhope Road, changed to Service 3 and continued via Tyne Dock back to Market.

Based on an original by G. Burrows dtd April 1971
Additional data supplied by S. Lockwood
Drawn by R.A Smith April 2007 No 791 (v5)

A Before 1957 / After 1957

B Before 1947 & after 1961 / 1947 to 1959

C From February, 1958

D Later layout

E From February, 1958

F After 1961

Depots: Upper Depot (1906) / Lower Depot (1925)

GEOGRAPHICAL SETTING

On the south side of the River Tyne, where it flows into the North Sea, lies the town of South Shields. Now part of the Metropolitan Borough of South Tyneside within Tyne and Wear, it was, until 1974, a County Borough within County Durham, having been granted this status in 1889. Like its neighbour Newcastle, seven miles upstream on the opposite bank of the Tyne, South Shields's prosperity was founded on coal and ship building, both now defunct. Tyne Dock was one of the major exporting outlets for the County Durham coalfield. Part of the town was settled in Roman times, a fort named Arbeia being established at the area now known as The Lawe. The present town has 13th century origins. In trolleybus days, the population was around 107,000.

HISTORICAL BACKGROUND

The electric tram system in South Shields, inaugurated in 1906, reached its peak in 1931 with 49 cars in operation. A compact pattern of services ran from the Market Place and Pier Head areas to Westoe, Chichester, Stanhope Road and Tyne Dock. In 1922, a new route was opened to King George Road, where the trams ran on a reserved track.

In the mid-1930s, the Corporation wished to expand its transport services into the rapidly developing housing areas in the south-east of the Borough. The South Shields Corporation Act 1935 empowered the Corporation to introduce trolleybuses on these new routes, as well as on the existing tram routes.

Thus, the first trolleybus service opened on 12th October 1936, using four vehicles. The initial route was from the Market Place via Laygate, Chichester, Mortimer Road and King George Road to Prince Edward Road, terminating at Fremantle Road, where a turning loop was provided. This was extended on 2nd May 1937 to Marsden Bay, overlooking the North Sea. The area beyond Fremantle Road was still undeveloped, and the main service continued to turn here, with only certain journeys in the summer continuing to Marsden Bay. The following day, 3rd May, the first tram route was converted to trolleybus operation, this being between the Market Place and Stanhope Road. In 1938, trolleybuses took over the remainder of the original tram system, with the Tyne Dock – Laygate – Pier Head route commencing on 11th April, followed by the Fowler Street to Chichester via Westoe section on 14th April. The King George Road tram route, for which a streamlined centre-entrance car had been purchased in early 1936, was retained for the foreseeable future.

Further development of the trolleybus system occurred in 1938, when the Coast Road service between Pier Head and Marsden Bay was opened for trolleybuses on 9th July, followed by a further extension of this service on 23rd July to Marsden Grotto. This latter provision was encouraged by the proprietor of the Grotto, who provided the land for the cliff top turning circle and a contribution of £150 towards the cost of the overhead wiring. The seafront section from Pier Head along Sea Road, Broadway and the Coast Road was wired using very neat Ohio Brass overhead equipment. The American manufacturer proudly advertised its involvement on this route as 'the trolley coach route under water', a reference to an area often shrouded in sea mist!

The outbreak of war halted any further plans to expand the system. South Shields suffered greatly from bombing raids, especially in the autumn of 1941. On 30th September, a raid destroyed three trolleybuses at the Market Place, although their chassis were salvaged and they re-entered service the following year with new bodywork. The Coast Road route and the Marsden Bay extension of the Prince Edward Road route from Fremantle Road were discontinued for most of the war. The Pier Head to Fowler Street section was also replaced by trams for a period in 1943. Increased passenger traffic caused by essential war work put pressure on the already depleted fleet. Second hand vehicles were sourced and consideration was even given to converting motorbuses, whose operation was reduced due to fuel shortages, to trolleybuses.

Powers under the Wartime Defence Regulations enabled new wiring to be erected in Centenary Avenue to allow a workers service to run from Horsley Hill direct to Tyne Dock. The operation commenced in September 1942, using one of the newly acquired second hand trolleybuses.

The immediate post-war priority was to replace the remaining trams on the King George Road route and this took place from 31st March 1946, when trolleybuses took over the route, initially operating to the Market Place. From 24th July 1947, the route was extended using new wiring along Mile End Road and Fort Street to serve The Lawe. The new wiring link in King George Road between Mortimer Road and Westoe for the Ridgeway service also allowed an all day service to be introduced between Horsley Hill, Centenary Avenue and the Market Place, in addition to the existing workers service from this area to Tyne Dock, introduced during the war.

The expansion of trolleybus services into the Horsley Hill area progressed further during 1948, when a service was introduced using new wiring from Westoe along Horsley Hill Road and Highfield Road to Horsley Hill Square on 5th January. From 28th March, this was extended to meet the Prince Edward Road route at the Marsden Inn shortly afterwards.

By 1950, the trolleybus system had reached its zenith, both in terms of size and patronage. There were 67 vehicles working over 16 miles/25.7km of route. Service numbers, which were displayed at the front of the vehicles, were brought into use about this time. The services operated were:

1	Stanhope Road–Chichester–Westoe–Pier Head
2	Tyne Dock–Laygate–Market Place–Pier Head
3	Tyne Dock–Laygate–Westoe–Fowler Street–Market Place
4	Stanhope Road–Chichester–Laygate–Market Place
5	The Ridgeway–Westoe–The Lawe
7	Horsley Hill–Centenary Avenue–King George Road–Market Place
8	Horsley Hill-Centenary Avenue-Chichester-Tyne Dock
9	The Lawe-Market Place-Trinity Church-Tyne Dock
10	Stanhope Road-Tyne Dock-Market Place-Pier Head-Coast Road-Marsden Grotto
11	Marsden Grotto-Marsden Inn-Prince Edward Road-Chichester-Market Place
12	Marsden Grotto-Marsden Inn-Highfield Road-Westoe-Market Place

Service 1 and 2 were linked between Stanhope Road and Tyne Dock to form a circular service.

Services 3 and 4 were linked between Tyne Dock and Stanhope Road to form a 'figure of eight' service.

Several other un-numbered special services operated at peak-hours for dock workers, to and from most parts of the system.

Service number 6 was never used as it clashed with that of a key South Shields to Newcastle bus service operated by the Northern General Transport Company.

The system continued largely unchanged up to 1957, when the decision was made to convert the highly scenic Coast Road service 10 to motorbus operation. Never economically viable with a 30 minute basic frequency, the high cost of maintaining the overhead on such an exposed route sealed its fate. The actual changeover took place unexpectedly. An unusually heavy snowfall on 7th February 1958, stranding trolleybuses on the Coast Road, proved the last straw and motorbuses took over the service permanently on 10th February, after the road had been cleared. Thus this service, opened as the 'trolley coach route under water', closed as the trolleybus route under snow! On the plus side, the much needed replacement of the pre-war trolleybus fleet was assisted by the purchase of ten second hand trolleybuses from Pontypridd and St Helens in 1957 and 1958.

However, by this time the neglected state of the trolleybus network was giving cause for concern. Observers report that the vehicles routinely had bent trolley poles with ragged strips of insulation tape flapping from them. Dewirements were common, even on straight stretches of wiring where its loose suspension caused oscillations which literally bounced the poles off the wires. At one stage the Ministry of Transport imposed a universal 20 mph/32 km/h speed limit over the whole system. However, by this time the neglected state of the trolleybus network was giving cause for concern. Observers report that the vehicles routinely had bent trolley poles with ragged strips of insulation tape flapping from them. Dewirements were common, even on straight stretches of wiring where its loose suspension caused oscillations which literally bounced the poles off the wires. At one stage the Ministry of Transport imposed a universal 20 mph speed limit over the whole system. In October 1959, the Transport Committee considered conversion to motorbuses but resolved to defer any such decision for two years, except that the workmens' service 9 would be converted immediately.

Impending roadworks decided the fate of the Ridgeway to The Lawe trolleybus service, which last ran on 2nd October 1961. The Marsden and Horsley Hill services 7, 8, 11 and 12 succumbed to motorbuses after 1st May 1963, followed on 29th April 1964 by services 1 to 4. That evening, the final trolleybus journey of all was operated from Pier Head to Stanhope Road. In the last two years of operation the services were operated by a mix of trolleybuses and motorbuses, with the latter being more prevalent as new vehicles were delivered. Thus the trolleybuses literally faded away after 27 years of service.

Abbreviations used in the captions:

AEC – Associated Equipment Company (Trolleybus chassis manufacturer)
BICC – British Insulated Callenders Cables Ltd (Trolleybus overhead wiring manufacturer)
SSCT – South Shields Corporation Transport

Note: The timetable extracts refer to services as at 1st May 1952, and the original wording as used by the Transport Department is reproduced.

Service No 1
Stanhope Road – Chichester – Westoe – Pier Head

MONDAY to FRIDAY

Depart Stanhope Road to Fowler Street only
5.50am 6.17am 6.47am 7.30am 7.45am 8.00am 8.15am 8.30am
8.45am 9.00am 9.15am 9.30am 9.45am

Stanhope Road to Pier Head
7.20am 7.37am 7.52am 8.07am 8.22am 8.37am 8.52am 9.07am
9.22am 9.37am 9.52am 9.59am 10.07am

and alternate 7 & 8 minutes until

7.07pm 7.12pm 7.21pm and every 9 mins until 10.21pm 10x30pm
10x39pm
X   Fowler Street only

Depart Pier Head
7.27am 7.42am 7.57am 8.12am 8.27am 8.42am 8.57am 9.12am
9.27am 9.42am 9.57am 10.13am 10.20am 10.28am

and alternate 7 & 8 mins until

7.20pm 7.25pm 7.34pm and every 9 mins until 10.34pm 10.43pm

SOUTH SHIELDS CORPORATION TRANSPORT
Trolleybus Route Chronology
1936 - 1968

---------- tramway in service
────────── trolleybus route opened on date shown
────────── trolleybus route in service
---------- trolleybus route closed on date shown

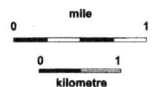

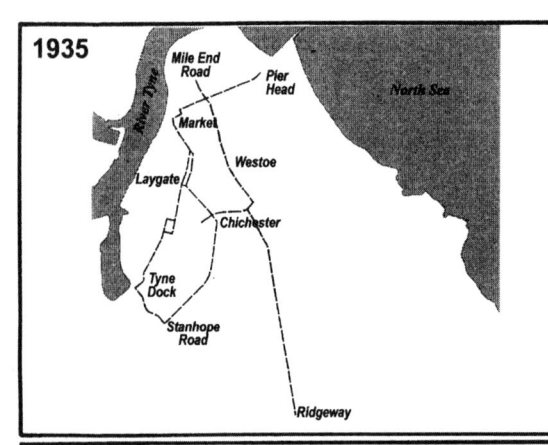

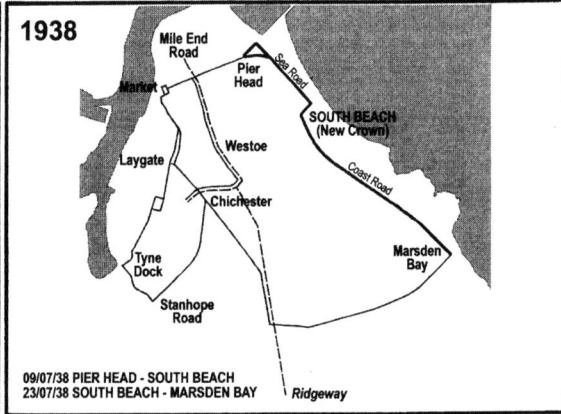

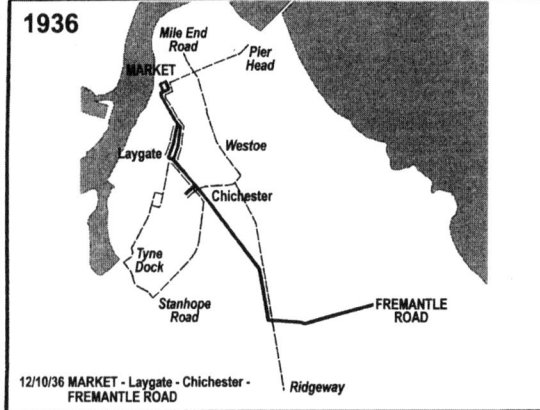

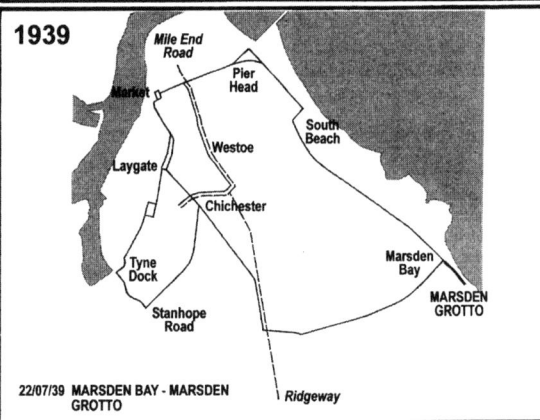

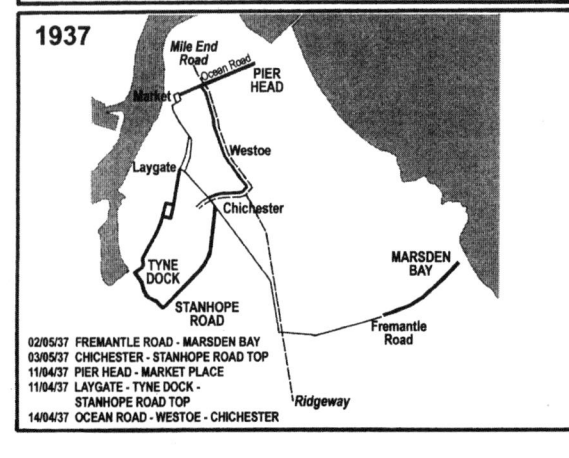

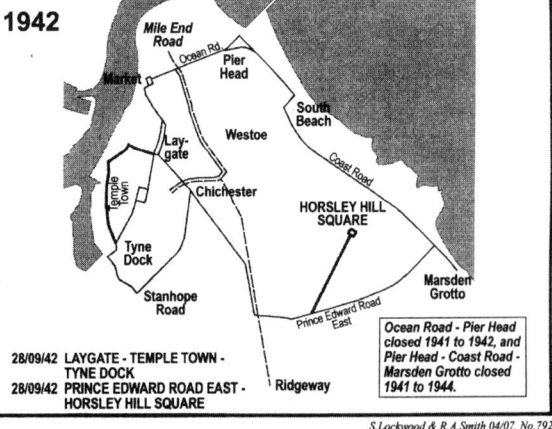

1935

1936
12/10/36 MARKET - Laygate - Chichester - FREMANTLE ROAD

1937
02/05/37 FREMANTLE ROAD - MARSDEN BAY
03/05/37 CHICHESTER - STANHOPE ROAD TOP
11/04/37 PIER HEAD - MARKET PLACE
11/04/37 LAYGATE - TYNE DOCK - STANHOPE ROAD TOP
14/04/37 OCEAN ROAD - WESTOE - CHICHESTER

1938
09/07/38 PIER HEAD - SOUTH BEACH
23/07/38 SOUTH BEACH - MARSDEN BAY

1939
22/07/39 MARSDEN BAY - MARSDEN GROTTO

1942
28/09/42 LAYGATE - TEMPLE TOWN - TYNE DOCK
28/09/42 PRINCE EDWARD ROAD EAST - HORSLEY HILL SQUARE

Ocean Road - Pier Head closed 1941 to 1942, and Pier Head - Coast Road - Marsden Grotto closed 1941 to 1944.

S.Lockwood & R.A.Smith 04/07, No.792

1946

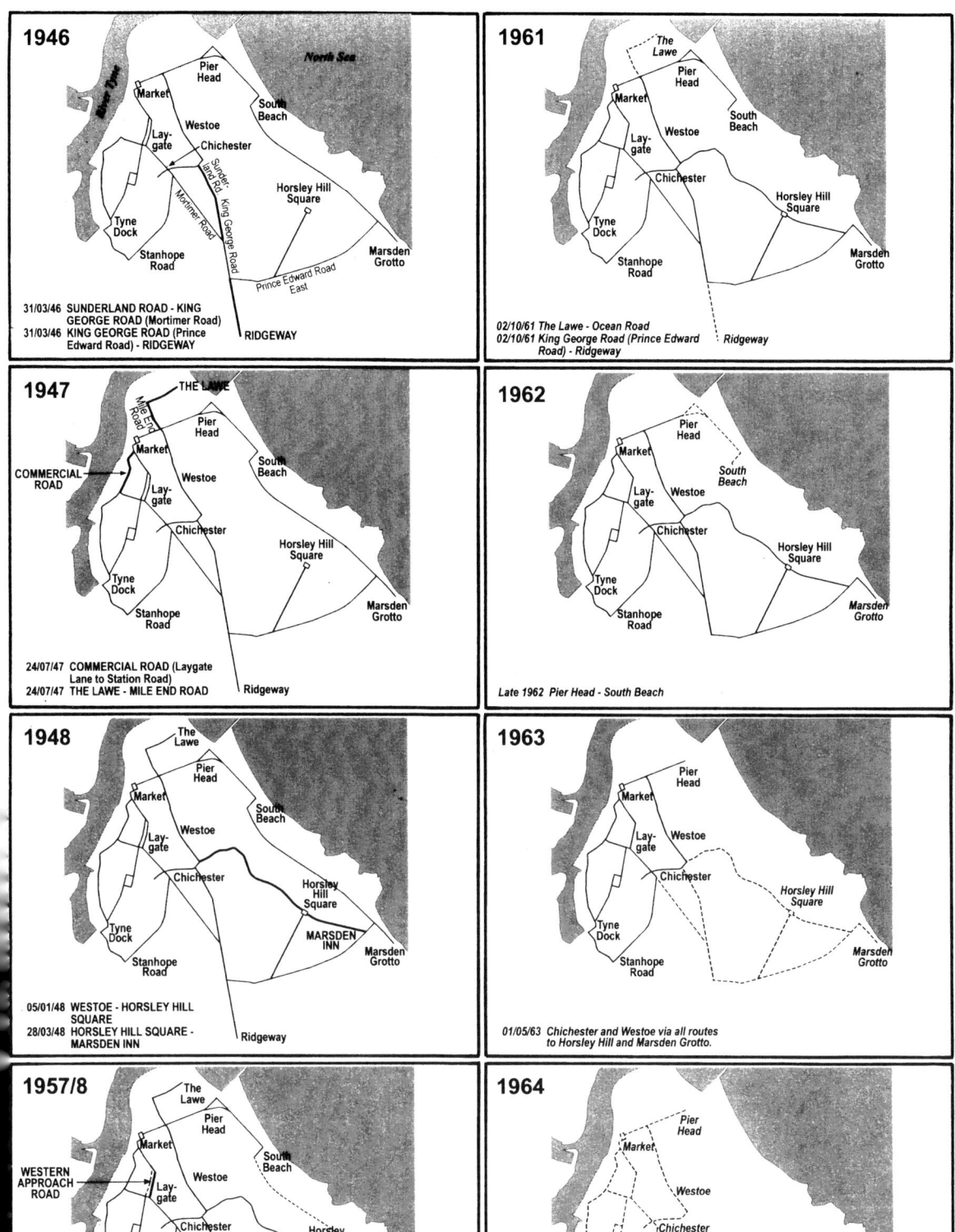

31/03/46 SUNDERLAND ROAD - KING GEORGE ROAD (Mortimer Road)
31/03/46 KING GEORGE ROAD (Prince Edward Road) - RIDGEWAY

1947

24/07/47 COMMERCIAL ROAD (Laygate Lane to Station Road)
24/07/47 THE LAWE - MILE END ROAD

1948

05/01/48 WESTOE - HORSLEY HILL SQUARE
28/03/48 HORSLEY HILL SQUARE - MARSDEN INN

1957/8

??/??/57 WESTERN APPROACH ROAD
09/02/58 South Beach - Marsden Bay

1961

02/10/61 The Lawe - Ocean Road
02/10/61 King George Road (Prince Edward Road) - Ridgeway

1962

Late 1962 Pier Head - South Beach

1963

01/05/63 Chichester and Westoe via all routes to Horsley Hill and Marsden Grotto.

1964

29/04/64 All remaining routes closed.

S. Lockwood & R. A. Smith 04/04, No 793

THE LAST TRAMS

1   Only one tram route survived the general conversion from trams to trolleybuses that occurred in the period 1936 to 1938, this being the Moon Street to King George Road service. This showpiece line, opened in 1922 included a 1 ½ miles/2.4km stretch along a reserved track on the median strip of the new dual carriageway road as far as the town boundary at The Ridgeway. Known as the 'gold-mine', the tram service continued throughout the war until finally succumbing to trolleybus operation in 1946, when the final nine trams were withdrawn. Car 44, one of the five 80 seat English Electric bogie cars built to open the service, is seen after the war on the reservation at the junction with Prince Edward Road. This point was known as Car Stop junction and the trolleybus wiring, where these vehicles bumped over the tramway after emerging from Prince Edward Road, is evident in the background. Following the end of the trams, the passenger shelter was moved to the edge of the roadway as seen in photograph 69. Some of the cars from this batch bore names in the late 1920s and early 1930s, although car 44 was not one of them. Car 45, for instance, was named *Monarch of Bermuda* after a ship built on the Tyne and was thus regularly seen 'sailing' along towards The Ridgeway. (AE Old)

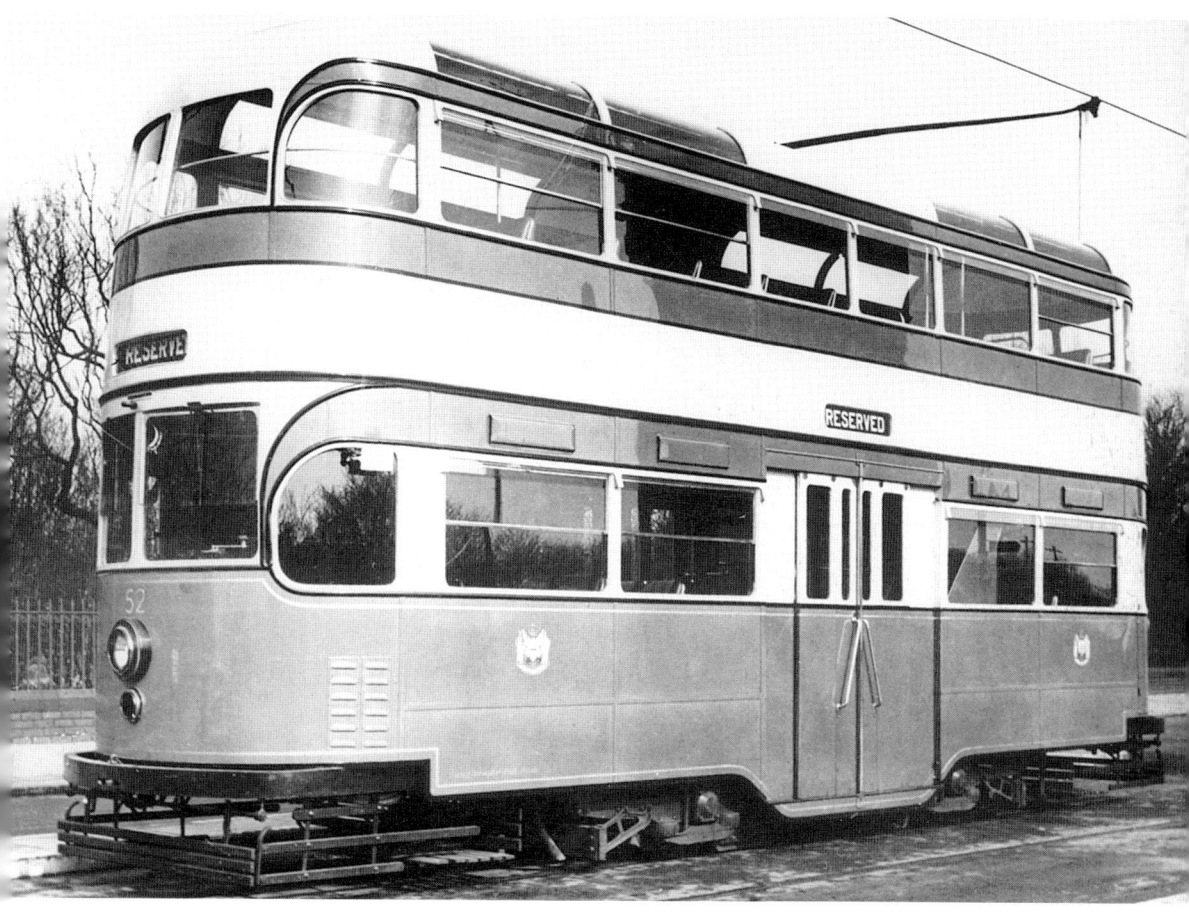

2 In 1936, the same year that the trolleybuses were introduced, the Tramways General Manager, ERL Fitzpayne, who later found fame at Glasgow, ordered this luxury streamlined tram for the King George Road service. Built by Brush, it had a Maley and Taunton swing-link four-wheel truck modified to accommodate a centre entrance body. The interior of the car was well appointed, including mirrors, diffused lighting and chromed steel fittings. Numbered 52, the car caused problems as it was very fast and therefore prone to catching up the car in front. It remained unique and was sold to Sunderland in 1946 running there until 1953. It is seen posed at Pier Head before entering service. (JS King collection)

THE FIRST TROLLEYBUSES

3   The opening of the system took place on 12th October 1936 when the crowds turned out to see the first vehicle, Karrier E4 200, being driven around the Market Place by the Mayor, Councillor E Hill, under the watchful eye of the local constabulary. The new operation had a distinctly Bradford look about it, this being evident in the livery style and other details such as stop signs. Even the motorbus stops shown on the right of this photograph were of Bradford pattern. (South Tyneside Libraries)

4   The first route operated to Prince Edward Road via Laygate and Chichester and ran alongside the trams in King George Road between Mortimer Road and Prince Edward Road. This early publicity shot shows 203, the last of the initial batch of four trolleybuses, unloading passengers in King George Road. (Author's collection)

PIER HEAD AND OCEAN ROAD

5   The Pier Head terminus of trolleybus routes 1 and 2 was adjacent to the memorial to Wouldhave and Greathead, inventors of the self-righting lifeboat. The vehicles turned behind the memorial and stood alongside it facing the town centre. The memorial is prominent in this view of 258 waiting to start a journey to Stanhope Road, with a St Helens vehicle behind on the Tyne Dock service. (DF Parker)

TYNE DOCK
2
SIGN OF SOUND VALUE AT YOUR CO-OPERATIVE STORE
204
CU 3593

STANHOPE ROAD
1
STANHOPE RD.
236
GNY 301

◄——— 6   Turning at Pier Head in 1959 is Karrier 204. The canopy just visible on the left is part of the Wouldhave and Greathead memorial, housing an early example of a self-righting lifeboat. 204 was later saved for preservation, as described in the captions to photographs 119 and 120. (JS King)

◄——— 7   A busy scene at Pier Head terminus, which was close to the seaside attractions and the beach. Those boarding ex-Pontypridd trolleybus 236 loading for Stanhope Road are about to experience sitting on the wooden seats on the top deck, which these former Welsh vehicles still retained. As can be seen, wiring extended beyond this point to the sea front, where an alternative turning point for Pier Head trolleybuses existed until the 1950s (see photographs 90 and 114). In addition, until 1958 a separate service number 10 operated beyond Pier Head along the Coast Road to Marsden Grotto. After this, some journeys on services 1 and 2 were extended beyond Pier Head along Sea Road on summer week ends and for special events. After 1962, all trolleybuses terminated at the Pier Head Memorial and the wiring beyond this point was removed. (RF Mack / Trolleybus Museum Company)

8   This is a pre-1958 view at the Pier Head showing 262 working service 10, having arrived at Pier Head from Marsden Grotto and the Coast Road. It is waiting behind 242 before proceeding. Service 10 ran to Stanhope Road via Tyne Dock. (RF Mack / Trolleybus Museum Company)

9	Looking westwards along Ocean Road, this view shows two trolleybuses, 258 and St Helens 207 which have just arrived at Pier Head and are waiting to turn at the terminal loop. (DF Parker)

10	A high-level view of Ocean Road, with 263 seen proceeding towards Pier Head. The windows of gift shops on the opposite side of the road seem to be attracting some attention. (J Copland / AD Packer)

FOWLER STREET AND WESTOE ROAD

11   At the western end of Ocean Road was a major road junction where Fowler Street, King Street, Mile End Road and Ocean Road met. Following the introduction of service 5 along Mile End Road to The Lawe in 1947, all these roads were used by trolleybuses. This resulted in the provision of a 'Grand Union' overhead wiring junction, allowing trolleybus access to each of the four roads from all the others. This was the only such trolleybus wiring junction in the country. The extent and weight of the fittings at this point resulted in the vehicles having to negotiate the junction with care to avoid a dewirement or becoming stuck on an insulated piece of wiring. This scene dates from 1953 and shows utility 250 having dewired and 'stopped the job'. Crews attempt to sort out the situation whilst trolleybuses (headed by 250's twin, 249) line up at the end of Ocean Road, unable to proceed. The delay has evidently caused passengers on 250 to abandon ship! The little used wiring connections from Ocean Road into Mile End Road, not required for use by normal services, are evident in this view. Also of note is the lack of a 'Shop at Binns' advertisement on the rear of 250. (J Copland / AD Packer)

12   Another view of the 'Grand Union' junction shows Karrier 227 about to cross the junction from Mile End Road into Fowler Street en route for The Ridgeway. The connections from King Street (on the left) into Mile End Road were used by peak hour service 9 workings to and from Tyne Dock and The Lawe. (J Fozard)

13   In the latter years of the system the wiring provision at this point was simplified due to the abandonment of the Mile End Road services. 267 is seen turning from King Street into Fowler Street in the 1960s, with Mile End Road, without trolleybus wires, in the background. (Author's collection)

14 Service 1 turned left from Ocean Road into Fowler Street, where it joined service 5 from Mile End Road and services 3, 7 and 12 coming from the Market Place via King Street. Ex-Pontypridd 239 is seen at the main stop in Fowler Street.
(DA Jones / London Trolleybus Preservation Society)

15   At the Town Hall, Fowler Street runs into Westoe Road. Although there was a wide carriageway at this point, the wiring was suspended using span wiring, producing a very neat effect. 248 is seen passing the Town Hall in 1963 en route to Stanhope Road. (JS King)

16   In Westoe Road, two trolleybuses are seen proceeding towards Westoe. 258 has just set off from the Mowbray Road stop, with utility 250 behind. The overbridge in the distance carried the Harton Colliery overhead electric railway to and from Westoe Colliery.
(RF Mack / Trolleybus Museum Company)

17   Near the top of Westoe Road, trolleybuses pass outside the Ingham Infirmary. On the right, 253 is proceeding towards Stanhope Road on service 1, despite the incorrect route number being displayed. Note the typical SSCT trolleybus stop sign on the left. These had black lettering on a yellow background and were similar to those used in Bradford. (J Fozard)

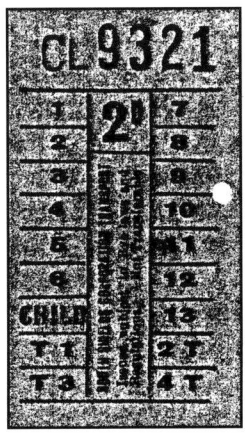

WESTOE

◄────── 18   At the Westoe Hotel, service 12 diverged, turning left into Horsley Hill Road, whilst the other routes turned right into Dean Road. The wiring junction included connections to allow service 12 vehicles returning to Depot from Marsden to cross directly into Dean Road. Utility 242 arrives at the Westoe Hotel on a journey from the Marsden Inn, and will turn right into Westoe Road. By 1959, this vehicle had been fitted with sliding ventilators to its side windows, replacing the half drop type that is evident in the view of the same vehicle at Pier Head (see photograph 8). Note the sign for the 'Westoe Towers' seamen's club, (Stella Maris), in the left background. (JS King)

◄────── 19   Following the abandonment of the Marsden routes in 1963, the wiring junction at this point was partially dismantled. This view shows one of the 1930s Karrier tower wagons undertaking this work, whilst St Helens 207 edges past as it turns into Dean Road. (Author's collection)

20   264 is seen turning from Dean Road into Westoe Road at the Westoe Hotel in 1963, after the abandonment of the Marsden routes. Note the partially dismantled overhead junction. (RF Mack / Trolleybus Museum Company)

21   This interesting scene dates from early April 1938. It shows Dean Road Westoe with Karrier 225 during a test run over the new trolleybus installation between Fowler Street and Chichester. This was the last section of the Stanhope Road/Tyne Dock routes to be converted to trolleybuses, being opened for traffic on 14th April. 225 can be seen having drawn up onto the kerb to allow traffic to pass. Note the tram and trolleybus overhead, an arrangement which would remain in use here until the end of the Ridgway trams in 1946, although the old tram poles would shortly be removed. w(JS King collection)

← 22 Taken on the same occasion as the previous view, this photograph shows the junction of Sunderland Road and Dean Road at Westoe. Note that a tram has now appeared in the background and the incomplete state of the trolleybus overhead. The tracks diverging to the right into Sunderland Road are those to King George Road and The Ridgeway. In 1946, at the same time as the final tramway abandonment, a roundabout was installed at this junction, together with a full circle of wiring for trolleybuses.
(South Tyneside Libraries)

23 Between Westoe roundabout and Chichester was this lay-by for trolleybuses, opposite the Regent cinema. Its purpose was to accommodate trolleybuses on special workings provided for late night film-goers leaving the cinema. Utility 244 pauses here on a Tyne Dock journey.
(J Copland / AD Packer)

CHICHESTER

24   The junction at Chichester was one of the major and busiest points on the trolleybus system. Known locally as 'the Chi', five roads converged here. Three of these carried trolleybus services, and a fourth provided the link to the depots in Dean Road, only a short distance from this point. Some of the most frequent services crossed the junction, these being nos 1, 3, 4, 11 and the peak-hour service 8. The roundabout was installed in 1949, and previous to this, the junction wiring was operated using point boys to ensure that each trolleybus gained the correct set of wires. This is a 1959 view of 213 crossing from Dean Road into Laygate Lane. Stanhope Road is on the right. (JS King)

→ 25   A short spur off Chichester junction along the western part of Dean Road led to the depots. 267 is seen parked on this section outside the Corporation Transport offices with the Chichester roundabout in the background. (I Alderson)

→ 26   Having negotiated the roundabout, St Helens 209 turns into Laygate Lane before stopping to pick-up waiting passengers opposite the Chichester Arms. The rather macho advertisement carried on its side would be frowned upon today. This area has since been substantially re-developed and is now dominated by Chichester station on the Tyne and Wear Metro system. (RF Mack / Trolleybus Museum Company)

8
267
SOUTH SHIELDS
CU 5279

ARMS
Wm YOUNGERS BEER
TYNE DOCK
3
men like CARLING LAGER BEER
CHEMISTS
209
BDJ 81

27   Looking in the opposite direction from the previous photograph, this is Laygate Lane with Laygate junction in the background. This section of wiring, between Chichester and Laygate, was used by the figure of eight services 3 and 4, and during one complete circuit, the vehicle would use these wires twice in the same direction. Thus the trolleybus seen in this photograph would have passed here on its outbound journey from the Market Place to Stanhope Road as service 4, then again, as seen here, on its return to the Market Place from Tyne Dock as service 3. On the left, behind the road sign, can be seen the trailing frog of the direct wiring connection from the upper depot, which ran along Beaufront Terrace to Laygate Lane. Utility trolleybus 250 is crossing the bridge over the Harton colliery electric railway, the trackbed of which is today used by the South Shields branch of the Tyne and Wear Metro. (J Copland / AD Packer)

SERVICE NO 3
TYNE DOCK – Laygate – Westoe – Fowler St - MARKET

MONDAY TO FRIDAY

Depart TYNE DOCK
6.55am 7.07am 7.18am 7.27am 7.34am 7.43am 7.50am 7.58am
8.07am and every 9 mins until 1134am 11.44am and alternate 7 & 8
Minutes until 6.59pm 7.04pm and every 9 mins until 10.22pm

Depart MARKET PLACE
5.25am 6.58am 7.07am (via Commercial Road) 7.14am 7.25am
7.30am 7.39am 7.48am and every 9 mins until 11.33am 11.41am
and alternate 7 & 8 minutes until 7.11pm 7.21pm and every 9 mins until 10.39pm

28 At the Chichester end of Stanhope Road, there was a turnout in the overhead wiring in advance of the junction of Stanhope Road and Mortimer Road, where service 11 diverged from the services 1 and 4. The short section of duplicated wiring is seen here in this view, dated 18th April 1952, showing 251 on service 11 about to proceed into Mortimer Road. The set of wires nearest the camera will bear right along Stanhope Road. (R Marshall)

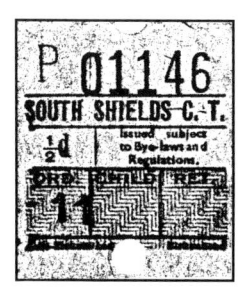

STANHOPE ROAD

← 29   Stanhope Road, served by services 1 and 4, ran for a distance of one mile to its junction with Boldon Lane. 254 is seen here pulling away from the stop at the Stanhope Hotel. (RF Mack / Trolleybus Museum Company)

← 30   The terminal point at Stanhope Road top is seen here. Trolleybuses arriving on services 1 and 4 turned right here into Boldon Lane and ran down to Tyne Dock to return to the town centre as services 2 and 3 respectively. Standing at the busy terminal stop here is St Helens 205, with 264 behind. In the background is Wrights biscuit factory, home of Wrights Fig Rolls and Ginger Snaps. (J Copland / AD Packer)

31   Karrier 226 is seen turning from Stanhope Road into Boldon Lane, with a passenger doing the "trolley tango" - taking advantage of the low speed to hop off the back – a common practice at the time. This view shows well the use of tramway style hangers in the overhead wiring which was typical of the South Shields system. (RF Mack / Trolleybus Museum Company)

32   This is the official alighting point in Boldon Lane at Stanhope Road top opposite Belle Vue Terrace. Ex Pontypridd 239 unloads passengers at the side of the wide carriageway in 1959. Latterly, there was no provision to turn trolleybuses here, although originally there was a full circle of wiring which was used to turn vehicles on service 10 (Stanhope Road–Tyne Dock–Coast Road). The provision was reduced in the late1950s to allow turning from the Stanhope Road direction only, but even this was later dispensed with. The motorbus on the left is operating a service from this point to Henderson Road, passengers transferring to the trolleybus services here. (JS King)

33   This interesting wartime view shows Karrier 208 at Boldon Lane (Belle Vue Terrace), just before it turns left into Stanhope Road. Part of the circle of wiring can be seen in the top left of the photograph. (WJ Haynes)

34   A view looking down Boldon Lane from Belle Vue Terrace, showing the width of the road and the site of the former wiring circle. In 1963, St Helens 207 stands alongside the Daimler motorbus operating the feeder service to Henderson Road. This service was a direct descendent of that inaugurated by battery-electric buses in July 1914. (CW Routh / AD Packer)

SERVICE NO 4
STANHOPE RD (TOP) – Chichester – Laygate - Market

MONDAY TO FRIDAY

Depart STANHOPE ROAD
5.45am 6.12am 6.39am 6.55am 7.01am 7.09am 7.17am 7.26am
7.35am 7.44am 7.52am and every 9 mins until 11.19am 11.26am
and alternate 7 & 8 mins until 7.03pm 7.07pm and every 9 mins until 10.25pm

Depart MARKET PLACE
6.40am 6.53am 7.03am 7.13am 7.19am 7.27am 7.34am 7.44am
7.52am 8.01am 8.10am 8.18am and every 9 mins until 11.45am
11.55am 12.05am and alternate 7 & 8 mins until 7.12pm
7.25pm and every 9 mins until 10.32pm 10.42pm

35 Trolleybuses reached Tyne Dock from Stanhope Road via Boldon Lane and Hudson Street. Boldon Lane is crossed by the railway at Tyne Dock Station, where St Helens 207, proceeding towards Stanhope Road, can be seen having just negotiated the overbridges at this point Between the bridges on the right behind the vehicle is the arched pedestrian entrance to the station, which today still gives access to the Metro system. (RF Mack / Trolleybus Museum Company)

(top right) 36 For most of the life of the trolleybus system, the Tyne Dock area was a grim place, the main street, Slake Terrace, being surrounded on one side by warehouses and the other by shops, pubs and boarding houses. In 1959, ex-Pontypridd 237 has emerged from Hudson Street and is negotiating the roundabout where a full circle of wiring was provided. In the distance can be seen the Arches, the long tunnel of bridges which carried the multi-level mineral railway tracks to the coal staiths in the dock. It was through these arches that, until 1929, the trams of the Jarrow and District Electric Tramways emerged to terminate at Tyne Dock. This was a company tramway, owned by the British Electric Traction group, and through running to South Shields Pier Head was achieved for two short periods, the last ending in 1927. A surviving Jarrow traction pole, complete with BET wheel & magnet emblem, can just be seen in this view immediately to the right of the Arches entrance. (JS King)

(right) 37 The dismal nature of Tyne Dock is evident in this 1963 view of 263 at the terminal stop. Vehicles departing from here on service 3 for the Market showed 'Westoe', presumably to encourage Market Place passengers to use the more direct service 2. After reaching Laygate, inbound service 3 vehicles showed the proper 'Market' destination. (CW Routh)

TYNE DOCK

38   This is the other side of Slake Terrace at Tyne Dock, with its line of pubs and boarding houses. Karrier 223 is seen here in 1959, when the properties were awaiting demolition.
(J Copland / AD Packer)

→ 39   Slake Terrace was re-developed in the early 1960s, and this transformed the look of the area. Having arrived here as a service 3, utility 244 pauses at the Tyne Dock stop before proceeding via Hudson Street and Boldon Lane to return to the Market Place via Stanhope Road as service 4. In the background is the Tyne Dock Hotel on the corner of South Eldon Street (to the right) and Templetown (to the left). Service 2 and 3 used South Eldon Street, and the peak hour workmen services serving Tyne Dock used Templetown.
(CAL Wright / CW Routh)

→ 40   Between South Eldon Street and Laygate, there was a short stretch of parallel running in separate streets. Trolleybuses proceeding to Tyne Dock ran from Laygate via Frederick Street and Gilbert Street to South Eldon Street. In the opposite direction they ran from South Eldon Street via Bertram Street to Frederick Street. This view looks east along Gilbert Street, with the wires turning out from Frederick Street in the background. St Helens 205 turns into South Eldon Street on a service 2 working, erroneously showing service '1'. Originally there was a wiring connection here turning right out of Gilbert Street allowing vehicles to return to Laygate, but this link disappeared during the 1950s. (JS King)

MARKET
4
244
CU 4605
KEEP LEFT
EVANS LTD

TYNE DOCK
MUSIC CENTRE
205
BDJ 77

41   This is a late 1930s scene at the northern end of the one-way section, showing the junction of South Frederick Street and Bertram Street looking towards Laygate. The northbound wiring can be seen turning out of Bertram Street on the left, to rejoin the southbound wires, whilst Karrier 201 proceeds along South Frederick Street towards Gilbert Street. Note the wiring suspension used here, which is of the single-drop catenary type. No trace of this part of Frederick Street now exists, and today the street ends at the Eureka public house, which is the large building behind the trolleybus in this view.(*Newcastle Chronicle and Journal*)

SERVICE NO 2
TYNE DOCK – Laygate – Market – PIER HEAD

MONDAY to FRIDAY

Depart TYNE DOCK to FOWLER ST ONLY
5.45am 6.19am 6.28am 6.46am 6.56am 7.12am 7.25am
7.40am 7.55am 8.10am 8.25am 8.40am 8.55am 9.10am
9.25am 9.40am

TYNE DOCK to PIER HEAD
7.04am 7.16am 7.33am 7.48am 8.03am 8.18am 8.33am
8.48am 9.03am 9.18am 9.33am 9.48am 9.55am and alternate
7 & 8 mins until 7.02pm 7.08pm and every 9 mins until 10.26pm

PIER HEAD
5M59am 6M20am 7.18am 7.33am 7.48am 8.03am 8.18am 8.33am 8.48am 9.03am
9.18am 9.33am 9.48am 10.03am 10.11am and alternate 7 & 8 mins until 7.26pm 7.30pm
and every 9 mins until 10.30pm 10.39pm

M – Depart MARKET PLACE

LAYGATE AND WESTERN APPROACH

42   At Laygate, there was an important junction of trolleybus routes with connections to Chichester, Tyne Dock, the Market Place and Commercial Road. This early post-war scene looks south-east towards Chichester and trolleybus 230 can be seen picking up passengers. North of this junction, the original arrangement, as seen here, was that trolleybuses ran in separate streets in each direction. Northbound, they used Green Street and Cuthbert Street, whilst in the southbound direction, Adelaide Street was used. On the left are the wiring connections into Green Street and out of Adelaide Street, and to the right are the wires leading into Frederick Street towards Tyne Dock. (*Shields Gazette*)

43   The layout at Laygate junction was altered in late 1958 when the first phase of the new Western Approach road opened. The construction of this road resulted in the demolition of much of the former housing and streets in the area. Trolleybuses on services 2, 4 and 11 now reached Laygate from the Market Place direction from the farther end the Allens store building seen on the left instead of the former wiring in Green Street and Adelaide Street. In 1959, 257 is about to turn into Frederick Street towards Tyne Dock, closely followed by utility 249. (JS King)

44   Seen here is a 1939 view of Green Street, looking from Laygate with the single direction wiring in view. A trolleybus can be seen in the distance. The former tramway poles, with cast iron bases and ball and spike finials, have been retained to support the trolleybus wiring.
(South Tyneside Libraries)

45	Laygate is in the background to this 1963 view of 254 at the southern end of Western Approach. Allens store is prominent on the corner of Laygate. The vehicle is proceeding towards the Market Place on service 4, the destination display having not been altered after the previous journey. (RF Mack / Trolleybus Museum Company)

46	This is a view of Western Approach near Laygate. The new road was dual carriageway, which necessitated the wiring being supported by bracket arms in each direction, using modern fittings. Utility 242, proceeding south towards Tyne Dock is shown outside Laygate Flats.
(RF Mack / Trolleybus Museum Company)

47   This 1961 scene is near the northern end of Western Approach and shows 204 pausing in the lay-by at one of the stops. In the left background is the former Pavilion Cinema at Derby Street, which was closed in 1959 and demolished in the early 1960s. The low building on the right is the John Collier clothing factory. (JS King)

48   Between the north end of Western Approach and the Market Place, the trolleybuses traversed Station Road. This is the junction of Station Road and Commercial Road, where the wiring for the peak-hour works services, including service 9, diverged. 247, one of the trio of Northern Coachbuilders bodied Karriers delivered in 1947, prepares to negotiate the roundabout that was latterly provided at this junction. It is nearing the end of a service 11 journey from Marsden, and the destination blind (but not the number display) has already been turned in readiness for its next journey from the Market Place which will be on service 12 to Marsden via Horsley Hill. The Commercial Road wiring runs off at the top left of this view. (J Fozard)

COMMERCIAL ROAD

49   Returning to Tyne Dock, we now look at the alternative route from here to the Market Place and Chichester via Templetown and Commercial Road. This was used by several peak hour services to accommodate shipyard workers. Two of these services were given numbers, no 8 from Tyne Dock to Horsley Hill via Chichester and no 9 to The Lawe via the Market Place. Added to these, many special un-numbered workings were also operated. Standing at Tyne Dock is utility 244, before it turns at the Tyne Dock circle and operates to Horsley Hill as service 8. The overhead wiring here uses London style BICC fittings. The redevelopment of this area is evident, including the modern flats on the skyline. (RF Mack / Trolleybus Museum Company)

Additional peak-hour services (service number not shown on vehicles)
(13)   Tyne Dock–Commercial Road–Laygate-Westoe-Highfield Road-Marsden Inn.
(14)   Templetown (River Street)-Tyne Dock-Stanhope Road-Chichester.
(15)   Tyne Dock-Commercial Road-Laygate-Chichester-Mortimer Road-
           Prince Edward Road-Marsden Inn.
(17)   Tyne Dock-Commercial Road-Laygate-Chichester-Westoe-Fowler Street-
           Market Place.
(18)   Tyne Dock-Commercial Road-Laygate-Chichester-Stanhope Road (Top).

50   The overhead wiring leading to Templetown and Commercial Road, which was used by services 8, 9 and works specials, diverged from the regular Pier Head routes near the end of South Eldon Street. Here, 248 negotiates the junction frogs. The Templetown wires run off in the upper centre of this view. Note that the unusually shaped cabin on the pavement behind 248's platform is a South Shields Police Box. (RF Mack / Trolleybus Museum Company)

51   On 22nd March 1964, in the final weeks of operation, the Omnibus Society hired utility 244 for a tour of the system, during which all available wiring was covered. The vehicle is seen here in Commercial Road using the wiring provided for peak hour workings. (R Rossiter)

Service No 8
HORS HILL SQ – Cent Ave – Chi – TYNE DOCK

MONDAY to SATURDAY

Depart HORSLEY HILL SQUARE
5.35am 6.30am 7.05am 7.30am 8.35am 12.38pm (NOT SATURDAY)
5.30pm TO TRINITY CHURCH ONLY (NOT SATURDAY)

Depart TYNE DOCK
6.00am 6.47am 8.00am 12noon (NOT SATURDAY) 5.00pm
5.30pm (NOT SATURDAY) TRINITY CHURCH 6.00pm (NOT SATURDAY)

SUNDAYS and PUBLIC HOLIDAYS – NO SERVICE

Service No 9
THE LAWE – Trinity Church – TYNE DOCK

MONDAY TO SATURDAY

Depart THE LAWE
7.07am (Motorbus) 7.43am 8.13am 8.43am 12.13pm 12.43pm
1.13pm 1.43pm NOT SATURDAYS 3.13pm (School Days only)

DEPART TYNE DOCK
7.27am 7.57am 8.27am (8.57am School Days ONLY) 12.00 noon
12.27pm 12.57pm 1.27pm (NOT SATURDAYS) 5.13pm 5.27pm
(NOT SATURDAYS)

52   At the junction of Commercial Road and Laygate Lane, the wires diverged with service 9 continuing along Commercial Road to Station Road and service 8 turning right into Laygate Lane to proceed towards Laygate junction and Chichester. As can be seen in this view looking towards the River Tyne, a full circle of wiring was provided here. This point was shown in timetables, for peak-hour journeys turning here, as 'Trinity Church'. Commercial Road runs across from left to right with Laygate Lane in the foreground. (JS King)

53   Between Commercial Road and Laygate junction, trolleybuses on works services passed under the main line railway at High Shields Station. Immediately before this, and between the station and Trinity Church, was a level crossing with the High Staiths branch of the Harton Colliery electric railway. The railway used locomotives which obtained power from overhead wires. Although both the railway and the trolleybus operated at 550 volts DC, a special arrangement was provided here where the wiring of each system crossed. This is shown here, with three section insulators placed in each of the trolleybus running wires to create a long dead section. Thus the electric railway had a continuous power supply at the crossing. Interestingly, the whole of the crossing wiring installation, including the trolleybus

wiring, was maintained by the Harton Colliery Company (later the National Coal Board), probably the only instance of such an arrangement on a British trolleybus system. Note the wiring circle at the junction with Commercial Road, shown in the previous photograph, in the background to this view dated 1945. The locomotive, number E3 in the Harton Colliery fleet, was built in Germany by Siemens in 1909 and ran until 1969. The railway branch to High Staiths outlasted the trolleybus system, finally closing in February 1976. The National Coal Board purchased several items of redundant trolleybus materials from the Corporation in the 1960s, for use on the Harton system. These included traction poles, overhead fittings and substation equipment. (Tyne and Wear Museums)

MARKET PLACE AND KING STREET

54   From the Station Road direction, trolleybuses entered the Market Place via Church Row. Here, 251 is on an outbound journey, passing Pontypridd 239 which is about to turn left into the Market Place. 251 is about to pass under a positive and negative power feeder in the overhead wiring. The prominent building, which occupies the south side of the Market area, is St Hilda's Church. (RF Mack / Trolleybus Museum Company)

→ 55   A busy, and very typical scene at the west side of the Market Place outside Barbours store. The wiring layout meant that trolleybuses had to lower their poles to allow following vehicles to pass, a process being enacted here. 270, with St Helens vehicles in front and behind, is on service 12 and will have arrived at the Market as a service 11 working via Laygate, the two services interworking across the Market Place. (RF Mack / Trolleybus Museum Company)

→ 56   An interesting photograph showing trolleybuses alongside the Barbours store. 269, which entered service in 1950, is seen when new on 24th June of that year. Behind, still in the pre-war lined out livery, is Karrier 215, which would be withdrawn a few months later. Barbours premises were demolished in the early 1960s. The company, still based in the town, is now world famous for the manufacture of waxed jackets. (R Marshall)

TYNE DOCK
R.RODGERS
MARSDEN STADIUM
12
CIRCUS
270
CU5282

Ideal Milk
MARSDEN VIA STADIUM
12
SOUTH SHIELDS
269
CU 5281

57   Taken on the same occasion as the previous photograph, this portrait of pre-war Karrier 233 shows it in original livery and before the fitment of a route number display. It is standing at the west side of the Market Place, outside the Norfolk and Suffolk Hotel, which was one of the few buildings to survive the bombing. (R Marshall)

⟶ 58   This is the scene in the Market Place following the German bombing raid on 30th September 1941. Trolleybuses 231 (left) and 203 stand wrecked on the east side of the square. The opening into King Street and the remains of Croftons department store are on the left. Further along the east side lay the remains of Daimler 234. All three vehicles were put back into service with new bodies in 1942. (South Tyneside Libraries)

⟶ 59   Standing at the same spot as the hapless trolleybuses in the previous photograph is 200. This is not quite the vehicle that is shown opening the system in photograph 3, but a hybrid assembled in 1952 using the body from the original 200 and the chassis from 205. It lasted until 1962 in this form, when it was withdrawn following an accident in the depot. Note the Tram Hotel on the right and the wiring coming round from King Street in the background. (CW Routh)

GRAPES HOTEL

TRAM HOTEL
SHIELDA WALLPAPERS
THEY ALWAYS PLEASE
BRUCE & HALL
FREDERICK ST.
200
CU 3589

60   The dramatic effect of the wartime destruction of the buildings around the square is evident in this early 1950s scene of the east side of the Market Place. The wiring layout allowed trolleybuses to pass those at the loading stands as can be seen here. King Street is in the left behind the vehicles. 259 on service 4 is ahead of utility 245 on service 2. (RF Mack / Trolleybus Museum Company)

→ 61   Rebuilding work is progressing in the background of this 1959 view, which co-incidentally shows the first (numerically) of both the batches of second hand vehicles which entered the fleet in the late 1950s. Ex-Pontypridd 236 leads, with St Helens 201 waiting to get access to the Marsden stop. In its home town, this vehicle had been the ceremonial last trolleybus on 1st July 1958. (JS King)

→ 62   A busy scene on the east side after the rebuilding of the area. Utility 244 loads for Stanhope Road on service 4. It is standing outside the Mermaid's Tale, which was the successor to the Tram Hotel, visible in photograph 59. The prominent building in the left background is the Old Town Hall. (Roy Brook)

MARSDEN INN
11
201
BDJ 74
FOX'S GINGER BISCUITS
STANHOPE ROAD
4
236
GNY 301

STANHOPE ROAD
4
FOX'S GINGER BISCUITS
7
244
CU 4605

63 Utility 250 negotiates the south side of the Market Place having just commenced a journey to Marsden via Laygate. In the background are vehicles on the stands for services 11, 2 and 4 on what was obviously a market day. (J Fozard)

→ 64 Seen turning from the Market Place into King Street in 1963 is St Helens 203 at the start of its journey to Tyne Dock via Westoe and Laygate.
(CW Routh / AD Packer)

→ 65 South Shields's main shopping street is King Street, which leads eastwards from the Market Place towards Fowler Street and Ocean Road. 261 is seen approaching the Market Place having completed a journey from Horsley Hill on service 7. Today, inevitably perhaps, King Street is pedestrianised. (J Copland / AD Packer)

TYNE DOCK
3
203
BDJ 76
SOUTH SHIEL
SPORTS STADIUM
HCU 614

ODEON
MARKET
7
261
CU 5100
76
WMJ 363

66   Near its eastern end, King Street is crossed by this railway bridge close to South Shields station. Today, this carries the Tyne and Wear Metro light railway tracks. The trolleybus wiring was slewed partly over the pavement due to the restricted headroom. In October 1954, 221 passes under the bridge on its way to the Market Place and Tyne Dock. The Fowler Street junction is in the background. (J Copland / AD Packer)

KING GEORGE ROAD AND THE RIDGEWAY

67   The first part of the former reserved track tramway south of Westoe roundabout was in Sunderland Road. Here, with a storm brewing, St Helens 208 is seen returning from The Ridgeway. The Caldwell Road roundabout, where Sunderland Road diverges from the newer King George Road, is visible in the background. (J Copland / AD Packer)

68   A typical scene in King George Road in trolleybus days, shows the wide road with daffodils in flower on the former central tramway reservation, where the tram rails still lie buried under the soil. 256 is en route for Marsden Grotto in April 1963, a few weeks before the cessation of trolleybuses on this road. (J Copland / AD Packer)

69   The junction of King George Road and Prince Edward Road is seen here, with utility 250 about to turn left into Prince Edward Road on service 11. This point was known as Car Stop junction. After the Ridgeway service was abandoned in 1961, a roundabout was constructed at this point, resulting in a revised overhead layout. Note the former tram passenger shelter, seen in photograph 1, has by now been re-located from the tram reservation to the roadside. (J Copland / AD Packer)

→ 70   The terminus of the King George Road route was at The Ridgeway, this being the name of a side road at this point, although the destination blinds always showed 'Ridgeway'. Utility 241 has just arrived at the terminus and will swing across the end of the former tramway reservation to return to The Lawe. In the distance can be seen a line of trolleybuses temporarily parked at the side of King George Road during the period of building alterations at the depot. (JS King)

71   During most of 1959, rebuilding work took place at the lower depot. Because of this, a large part of the trolleybus fleet was parked, when out of use, in King George Road between The Ridgeway terminus and Prince Edward Road. The trolleybuses, rather than motorbuses, were chosen for this treatment in order to minimise the noise nuisance for local residents. This is 223 at the head of the line of vehicles. (J Copland / AD Packer)

PRINCE EDWARD ROAD AND HORSLEY HILL

72   Having left the Ridgeway route at Car Stop junction, the trolleybus services along Prince Edward Road crossed Sunderland Road at Harton Nook, more commonly known as 'The Nook'. There were local shops here and 254 is seen pausing in the lay-by here en route to the Marsden Inn in 1959. (J Copland / AD Packer)

Service No 7
HORS HILL SQ – Cent Ave – King Geo Rd - MARKET

MONDAY TO SATURDAY

Depart HORSLEY HILL SQUARE
7.18am 7.32am 7.46am 8.00am 8.14am 8.28am 8.42am 8.54am
9.06am and every 15mins until 10.21pm 10.36pm (10.51pm & 11.06pm to CHICHESTER via MORT RD)

Depart MARKET PLACE
7.27am 7.39am 7.53am 8.07am 8.21am 8.35am 8.49am 9.05am
9.18am 9.31am and every 15mins until 10.30pm 10.45pm

73   From Prince Edward Road, trolleybuses reached Horsley Hill by way of Centenary Avenue. The first service to this area was introduced in wartime, being a direct route from Tyne Dock and later numbered 8. After the war it was joined by a route from the Market Place which became service 7. At the junction of Centenary Avenue and Prince Edward Road, a turning circle was erected at the end of the war. This proved awkward to negotiate and was subsequently removed. In April 1963, 268 proceeds along Centenary Avenue operating back to the Market Place from Horsley Hill. (J Copland / AD Packer)

74 Horsley Hill was the terminus of two services, the 7 from Market Place and the peak-hour service 8 from Tyne Dock, both arriving via Centenary Avenue. In addition, service 12 via Highfield Road passed through en route to Marsden via Marsden Lane. Trolleybuses turned by negotiating around the large central roundabout. Here St Helens 205 waits to depart on service 7 via Centenary Avenue in 1959. (JS King)

75 The square at Horsley Hill was dominated by the Horsley Hill Hotel, situated on the north-western side. St Helens 207 waits to depart on service 12 for the Market Place via Highfield Road, and will take the wires turning left in this view. The service 12 route between here and Westoe included a sharp right angle turn at the junction of Highfield Road and Horsley Hill Road near the stadium. This proved troublesome for trolleybus drivers to negotiate and was a prime spot for dewirements until 1953, when the radius of the curve was eased by the re-alignment of the road. (J Copland / AD Packer)

MARSDEN : INN, BAY AND GROTTO

76   The terminus of South Shields first trolleybus route was in Prince Edward Road at Fremantle Road. Here, the vehicles turned around a semi-circular island at the road junction. This facility was retained after the service was extended to Marsden, eventually being removed in the 1950s. This early post-war view shows 237, one of the trio of Bradford six-wheel trolleybuses purchased in 1945 standing at Fremantle Road. These vehicles, which retained their Bradford blue livery, were restricted to workings on this route. See photograph 105. (AE Old / R Marshall)

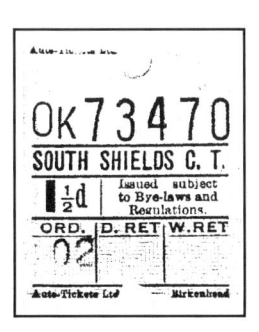

People love Player's
260
CU 4947
IN

MARKET VIA STADIUM
12
東山酒家 TUNG SHAN CHINESE RESTAURANT
202
BDJ 75
KEEP LEFT

← 77 Service 11 from Prince Edward Road, and service 12 from Horsley Hill shared a common terminus at the Marsden Inn roundabout. This turning facility was established in the mid-1940s, allowing the Fremantle Road service to be extended to here. 260 is seen performing the turning manoeuvre, with the Marsden Inn in the background. Note the wiring layout and the conductor behind the trolleybus pulling the handle for the frog. (J Copland / AD Packer)

← 78 St Helens 202, operating on service 12, negotiates the Marsden Inn roundabout. The conductor is running to pull the handle for the frog to enable the vehicle to return to Marsden Lane. (LW Rowe)

79 The terminal stop at Marsden for service 12 was in Marsden Lane, almost opposite the Marsden Inn. Here, 261 stands before returning to the Market Place via Horsley Hill. Bus crews all over the country will identify with this scene showing children pestering the conductor - 'Got any spare tickets mister?'. (J Copland / AD Packer)

80 Utility 242 stands at the service 11 terminal stop at the Marsden Inn, in this view looking towards the sea. Services 11 and 12 were worked as a linked service, vehicles from Marsden changing from service 11 to service 12 at the Market Place (or vice-versa). Arrivals at Marsden, however, returned via the same route on which the vehicle had arrived. (J Copland / AD Packer)

81 During the summer months, some journeys on the Marsden Inn services, (mainly, but not exclusively, service 11) were regularly extended down Redwell Lane to Marsden Grotto. This 1959 view shows utility 241 climbing Redwell Lane on its return from the Grotto. It is approaching the Marsden Inn with Marsden Bay and the North Sea in the background. (JS King)

82   At the bottom of Redwell Lane, the route passed under a bridge carrying the South Shields, Marsden and Whitburn Colliery Railway, a line linking Whitburn Colliery with the coal staiths on the River Tyne. A public passenger service was provided, known as the 'Marsden Rattler', which ran until 1953. In 1959, 269 is seen passing under the structure, which, during the war, incorporated air raid shelters in each abutment. The Marsden Inn turning circle can be seen through the bridge at the top of Redwell Lane. (JS King)

Service No 11
MARSDEN GROTTO / INN – Pr Ed Rd – Chi – MARKET

MONDAY TO FRIDAY

Depart MARSDEN GROTTO
9.20am 9.35am and every 15mins until 1035pm (10.50pm to CHICHESTER)

Depart MARSDEN INN
5.50am 6.20am 6.38am 6.52am 6.56am 7.07am 7.14am 7.18am 7.22am 7.29am 7.37am and alternative 7 & 8 mins until 10.29pm 10.37pm

Depart MARKET PLACE to MARSDEN INN
6.45am 6.52am 7.00am and alt 7 & 8 mins until 10.45pm

Depart MARKET PLACE to MARSDEN GROTTO
9.00am and every 15mins until 10.30pm

Service No 12
MARSDEN GROTTO / INN – Highfield Rd – Horsley Hill Road - MARKET

SUNDAY

Depart MARSDEN INN
9.35am 9.50am and every 15 mins until 11.05am 11.11am and alternate 7 and 8 mins until 10.33pm

Depart MARKET PLACE
9.48am 10.03am and every 15mins until 11.03am 11 11am and every 7 & 8 mins until 10.48pm

Extension to Marsden Grotto

Depart MARKET PLACE
11.03am 11.18am and every 15mins until 2.18pm

Depart MARSDEN GROTTO
11.24am and every 15 mins until 2.39pm

During the summer period the extension to MARSDEN GROTTO will be maintained to meet traffic requirements.

83   After passing under the bridge, service 11 and 12 trolleybuses turned right at the roundabout on to the A183 Coast Road (visible in the background to photograph 81). This roundabout was the original terminus of the Marsden service in 1937, designated Marsden Bay. In July 1939, an extension of just less than 1/3rd of a mile was wired to a purpose built turning area at Marsden Grotto. This was one of Britain's most spectacular trolleybus termini, being situated on the cliff top 95 feet above the sea. Here, a lift took patrons down to the Marine Grotto, a hostelry built into the cliff at shore level. Out in Marsden Bay itself, seabirds circled around Marsden Rock. 253 on service 12 is seen at the terminus with the lift to the Grotto visible on the left. The wording of the neon sign above the lift reads 'Marine Grotto', having been altered from the original 'Marsden Grotto' as seen in photograph 103. The neat construction of the Ohio Brass overhead wiring is evident here. (RF Mack / Trolleybus Museum Company)

COAST ROAD AND SOUTH BEACH

84   The Marsden Grotto terminus of the summer extension of services 11 and 12 was shared with the direct 'Coast Road' service 10 which ran all year round via the sea-front and Pier Head to the Market Place, Laygate, Tyne Dock to Stanhope Road Top. This was the first service to be abandoned, motorbuses taking over after 7th February, earlier than planned. Afterwards, the wiring was dismantled between Redwell Lane and the Mowbray Road turning circle. The scene shows 252, having just dewired whilst entering the Marsden Grotto turning circle. This incident followed a fast run along the Coast Road which had been experienced by the photographer, accompanied by Stanley King. Much of the Coast Road ran parallel to the South Shields, Marsden and Whitburn Colliery Railway, which ran in a cutting in the background of this 1954 view.
(J Copland / AD Packer)

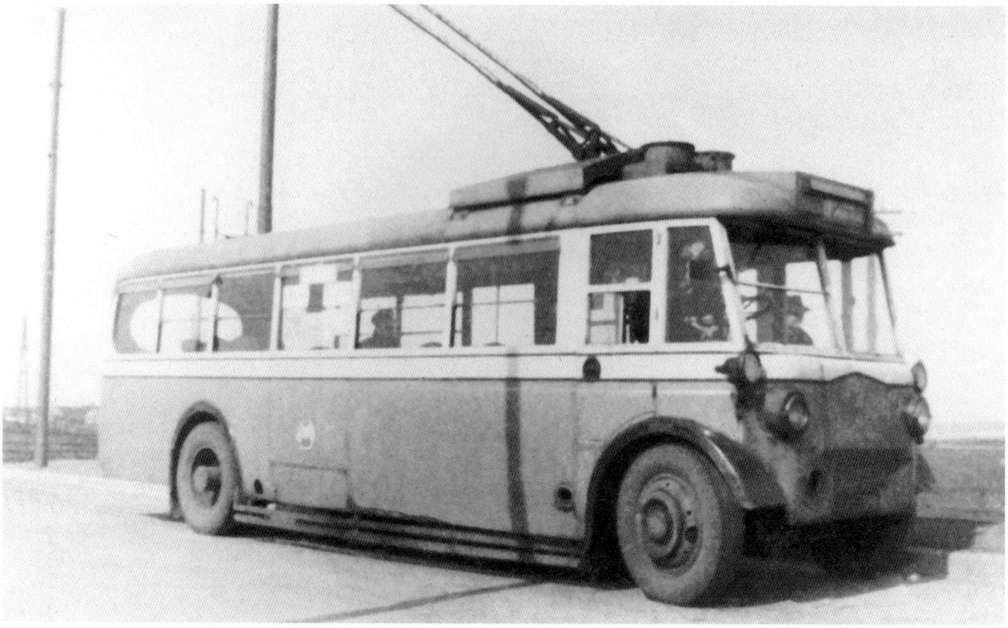

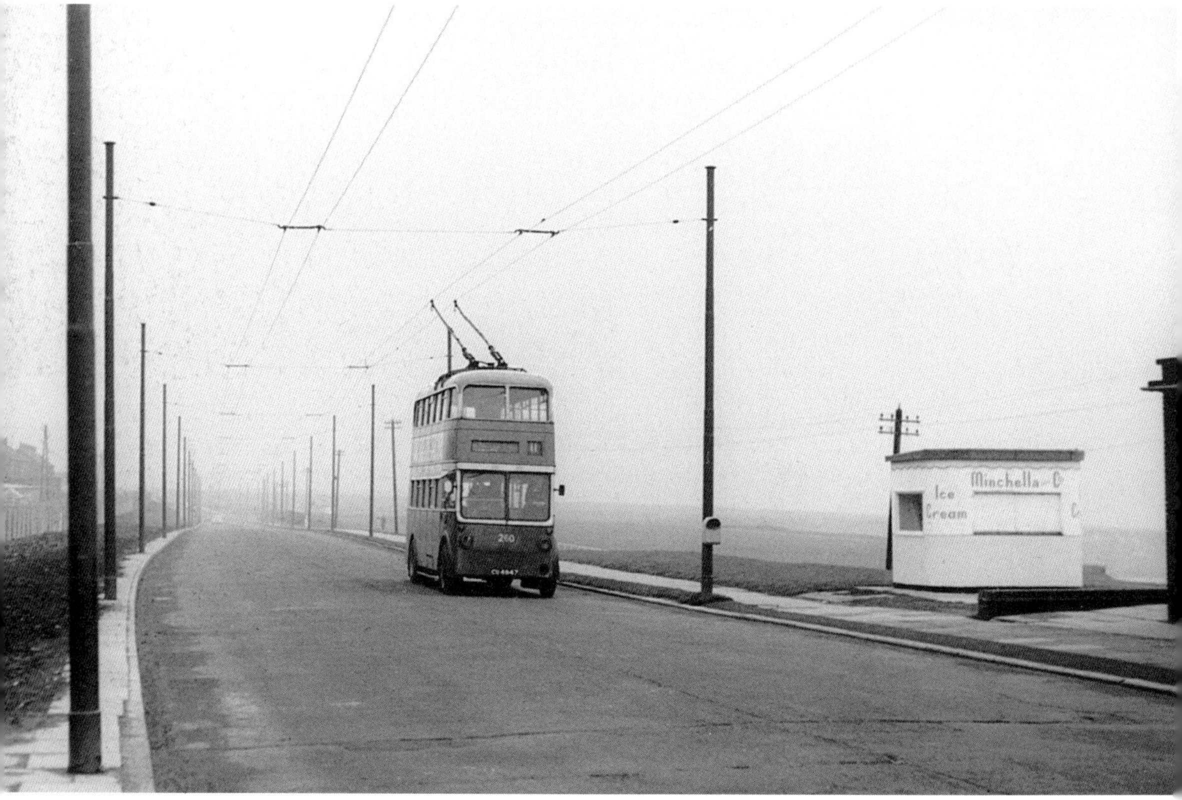
Minchella
Ice
Cream

← 85 Early post-war operation on the Coast Road service was typically in the hands of the 'odd' second-hand trolleybuses acquired during the war, including 236, the ex- Bournemouth Thorneycroft single-decker. This is seen in this rare view at Marsden Grotto.
(AE Old / R Marshall)

← 86 Because of wartime restrictions to seafront access, service 10 was discontinued in August 1941. Resumption came in 1944, initially restricted to operation at weekends only. Although this view actually shows the section between Redwell Lane and Marsden Grotto, it does give an indication of the operating conditions on the exposed Coast Road section between Marsden and Sea Road. 260, on service 11, is seen approaching the terminus. The Whitburn Colliery Railway, which had to be re-aligned a few yards inland when the Coast Road was built in 1929, is evident on the left.
(J Copland / AD Packer)

87 A turning circle was provided at the junction of Broadway and Mowbray Road at the New Crown Hotel. The portion of the route between here and Pier Head was retained for use in the summer months by trolleybuses on services 1 and 2 operating extended journeys beyond Pier Head. These workings were officially designated service 1A. Vehicles turned using the existing turning circle around a triangular island at the end of The Broadway, where 262 is seen performing the turn here in 1959. The former Coast Road route continued into the right background, along The Broadway.
(JS King)

SERVICE NO 10

STANHOPE ROAD – Tyne Dk – Pier Head – Coast Road – MARSDEN GROTTO

MONDAY TO SATURDAY

Depart STANHOPE ROAD
8.00am 9.00am and every 30 mins until 9.30pm 10.06 pm

Depart MARSDEN GROTTO
6.40am (To MARKET only) 7.10am 7.40am 8.25am and every 30 mins until 9.55pm 10.30pm

During the summer period this service will be augmented to meet traffic requirements.

88   Trolleybuses on the promenade. Sea Road turns onto the sea front a short distance north of the New Crown. 270 is seen rounding the curve on the approach to South Beach terminus. Note the unobtrusive Ohio Brass overhead fittings. In the background the white capped waves roll in from the North Sea. The South Pier can be seen, together with Tynemouth, across the Tyne estuary, in the far background. (J Copland / AD Packer)

89   St Helens 206 picks up passengers leaving a flower show at Bents Park in 1959, on its way to the Pier Head and Tyne Dock. For such events, the vehicles carried cards in the windscreen, on this occasion reading 'To and From Flower Show'. (JS King)

90   Nearing the Pier Head terminus in 1959, utility 241 is seen on the section of one-way wiring passing the Sea Hotel as it returns from South Beach. The turn back wiring, mentioned in the captions to photographs 7 and 114, which would have trailed in from the left of this view behind the vehicle, had been removed by this date. The remaining wiring beyond the Pier Head Memorial was removed in 1962. (JS King)

THE LAWE

91 The section of route between Fowler Street junction and The Lawe opened for traffic in July 1947. Throughout its life it was operated as a through service to The Ridgeway via King George Road. The unique Daimler utility trolleybus 234 is seen on a journey from The Lawe in Mile End Road at Bath Street, near the former Ridgeway tram service terminus at Moon Street. (DA Jones / London Trolleybus Preservation Society)

92 The trolleybuses turned right from Mile End Road into Fort Street to reach The Lawe terminus. Ex-Pontypridd 239 is seen arriving at the top of Fort Street at the terminus in 1959. The reversing wires can be seen in the top foreground of this view including the thick brass runner installation referred to in the next caption. (JS King)

Service No 5
THE RIDGEWAY – Westoe – THE LAWE

MONDAY TO SATURDAY

Depart THE RIDGEWAY to MARKET
5.20am 6.00am 6x19am 6.35am 6.55am 7.05am X NOT SATURDAYS

Depart THE RIDGEWAY to THE LAWE
7.27am 7.41am 7.55am 8.09am 8.23am 8.37am 8.51am 9.00am
and every 15 mins until 10.15pm 10.30pm

Depart MARKET PLACE to RIDGEWAY
5.40am 6.17am 6x37am 6.52am 7.12am 7.22am

Depart THE LAWE to THE RIDGEWAY
7.33am 7.47am 8.01am 8.15am 8.29am 8.43am 8.55am 9.07am
9.21am and every 15 mins until 10.21pm 10.36pm (10.51pm to WESTOE & CHICHESTER)

93   The Lawe is a headland at the mouth of the River Tyne and the North Sea and there are panoramic views from here across the water. The terminus was at the junction of Fort Street and Lawe Road, where vehicles reversed on Lawe Road across the end of Fort Street. This was the only example of a wiring reverser on the South Shields system. It was necessary because permission was refused to erect wiring on a roundabout at the junction of Lawe Road and Green's Place, a short distance to the north. The reverser was unusual in that brass runner, of greater thickness than normal copper wire, was used for the straight reversing section instead of normal running wire. Before reversing, St Helens 202 pauses for the conductor to walk back to operate the frog, a procedure described in the next caption. (RF Mack / Trolleybus Museum Society)

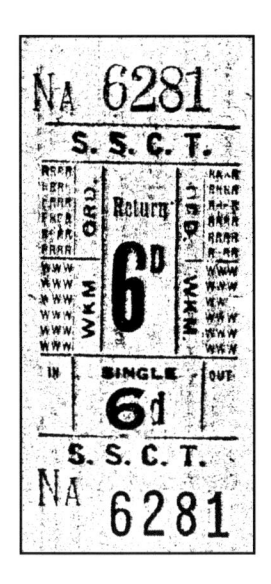

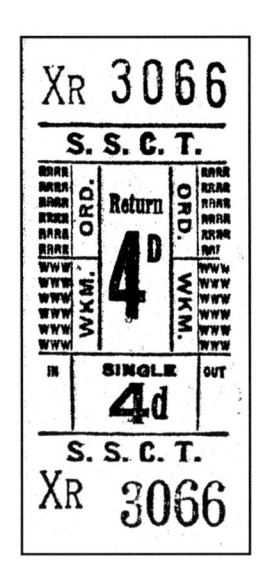

94 Instead of the usual spring-loaded type, a hand operated frog was used at the south end of the reverser to allow the trolley poles to reverse over the frog. Having reversed, 217 is ready to depart. It will turn left into Fort Street in front of the pillar box. In the far left background is the North Sea. (RF Mack / Trolleybus Museum Society)

DEPOTS

←——— 95   South Shields's trolleybuses were housed in two depots, which were adjacent to each other in the middle part of Dean Road near Chichester junction. Both buildings were sited parallel to Dean Road. The upper depot, nearest Chichester, was the original electric tram depot dating from the opening of the system in 1906. The entrance into the depot yard was via a narrow gateway. The depot itself had seven roads, three for vehicles entering and four for vehicles leaving. This photograph of three of the exit roads shows, from left to right, vehicles 253, 240 and 200. Note the tram rails still prominent in the yard. The Harton colliery electric railway, now the route of the Metro trains, ran alongside the eastern boundary of the depot. (DF Parker)

96   The upper depot building can be seen in this view dated October 1954, showing 206 and 270. The latter vehicle was the highest numbered trolleybus in the fleet.
(J Copland / AD Packer)

97   The lower depot, dating from 1925, was to the south-west of the original depot, the yard being immediately behind its back wall. The lower depot yard is seen here in October 1954, with Dean Road in the background. Note the tram rails. A line up of pre-war trolleybuses waits to enter the depot building with 213 at the head. (J Copland / AD Packer)

98   The entrance of the lower depot was rebuilt in 1959, a modern frontage being provided. The new arrangement is seen in this view of 212 emerging. The title of the undertaking can be seen displayed above the doorway. (RF Mack / Trolleybus Museum Company)

ROLLING STOCK

99   200 to 233 (CU3589 to 3596, 3850 to 3873, 3974, 3975)

This batch of 34 trolleybuses which formed the original fleet, had Karrier E4 chassis with Weymann composite 56 seat bodywork. They were delivered between 1936 and 1938 in three batches, 200 to 203 in 1936; 204 to 207 in 1937 and the remainder in 1937/8. The bodies of 203 and 231 were destroyed in an air raid in September 1941 and they were re-bodied as described in the next caption. The introduction of route numbers in 1950 resulted in all the existing fleet having a route number box fitted beside the front destination indicator. In 1952, the chassis of 200 was scrapped and the body placed on the chassis of 205, the complete vehicle then being numbered and registered as 200 (see photograph 59). During the 1950s 228 was fitted with sliding window ventilators instead of the half-drop type. The withdrawal of this batch was a protracted affair. 208 was the first in October 1950, quickly followed by 215, 219 and 222 at the end of that year. Six survived until 1963, these being 204, 212, 213, 226, 227, and 228. In the 1950s and 1960s these vehicles seem to have spent their time operating on services 1 to 5, being rarely seen on the Marsden and Horsley Hill routes. This is an official view of 205 before delivery.
(Author's collection)

100 **Karrier wartime rebodies**

As noted in the previous caption, the bodywork of these vehicles was destroyed by enemy bombing in September 1941. They were re-bodied by Weymann, re-entering service in 1942. The new bodies were of wartime utility specification, although the lower deck closely resembled the original Weymann product. The rear emergency exit on the upper deck was unglazed until after the war. In 1953 231 was decorated to commemorate the Coronation of Queen Elizabeth, and it toured the routes daily in service during this period (see photograph 114). Both vehicles were withdrawn from service in 1958. 203 is seen in the Market Place in the early 1950s. (AB Cross)

101 **234 (CWK 67)**

This former demonstration trolleybus was purchased in 1938. It had a Daimler CTM4 chassis (the first of this type to be built) and a Willowbrook 56 seat body. Since 1937 it had been demonstrated by Daimler in Derby and Newcastle in a red and cream livery. During this time it ran with the registration CWK 47, but entered service in South Shields as CWK 67. Presumably this was the correct number and the previous one had been displayed in error. Its life in this form was relatively short, as the body was destroyed in the bombing raid on the Market Place in September 1941. Its subsequent history is detailed in the following caption. Photographs of the vehicle in its original form are very rare, but this view shows it whilst on demonstration to Derby in September 1937. (R Marshall collection)

SOUTH SHIELDS CORPORATION
DOUBLE DECK 2 AXLE TROLLEYBUS

Chassis: Karrier E4.
Body: Weymann built 1936/38.
Fleet No. 201 - 233.

Scale: 4 mm = 1 Foot.

DRAWING No. TB69

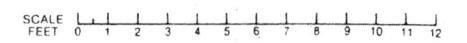

SCALE FEET 0 1 2 3 4 5 6 7 8 9 10 11 12

AVAILABLE FROM :- TERRY RUSSELL, "CHACESIDE", ST. LEONARDS PARK, HORSHAM, W. SUSSEX. RH13 6EG.

SEND 4 FIRST CLASS STAMPS FOR COMPLETE LIST OF PUBLIC TRANSPORT DRAWINGS.

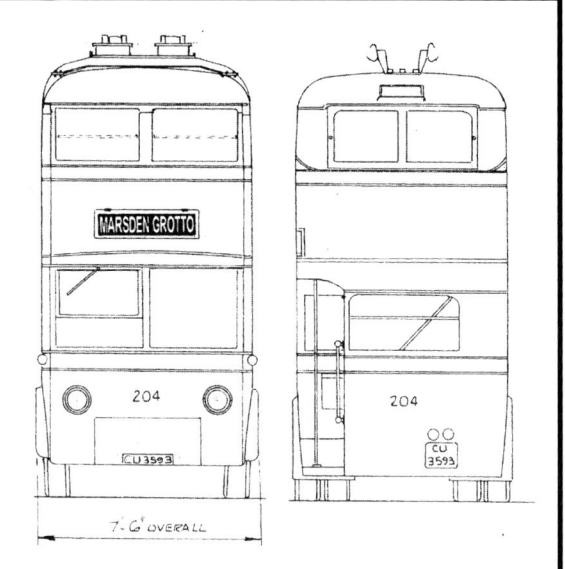

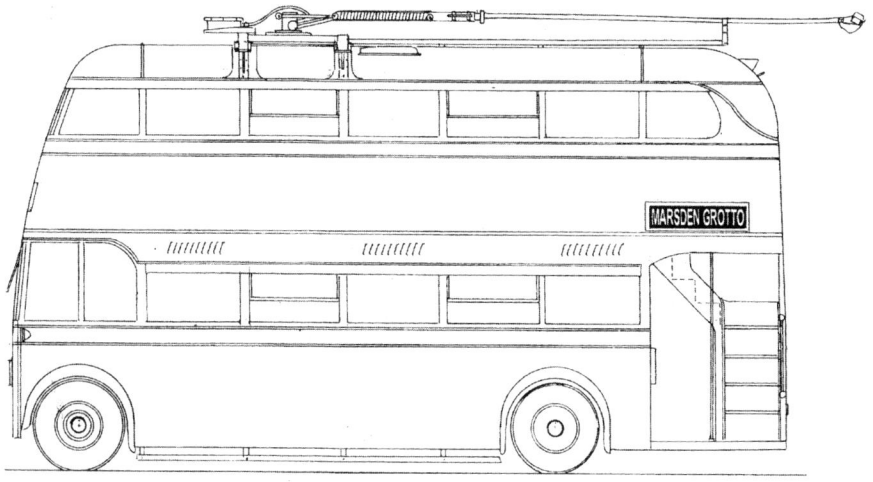

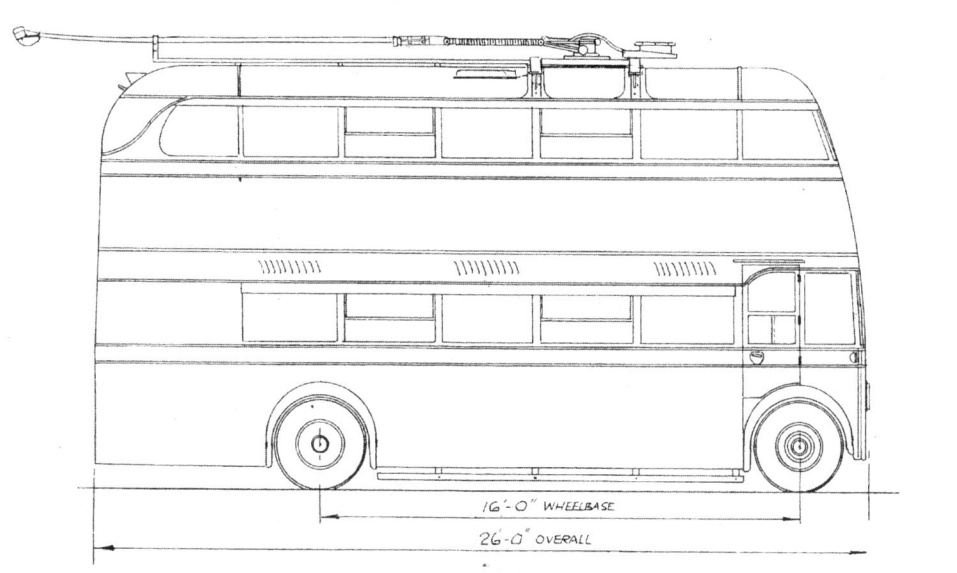

MARSDEN GROTTO

204

CU 3593

204

CU 3593

7'-6" OVERALL

MARSDEN GROTTO

16'-0" WHEELBASE

26'-0" OVERALL

102   In 1942, 234 re-entered service after being fitted with a new Roe body to utility specification. Like the other wartime rebuilds, an unglazed emergency exit at the rear of the upper-deck, later glazed, was originally included. The only other alteration was the fitment of a front route number display in 1950. The vehicle was withdrawn in 1958. It is seen here in the Market Place on 10th April 1943 in wartime grey livery, working on the Fremantle Road service. The brick structure to the left of the vehicle in front of the Old Town Hall was the entrance to an underground air-raid shelter. (South Tyneside Libraries)

103   **235 (KY 6210)**

The need for additional vehicles to cater for the increased passenger traffic due to the war resulted in the Corporation scouring the market for second-hand trolleybuses. The first to appear was this AEC Q type double decker (type designation 761T) which was purchased from Bradford in 1942. New in 1934, and known as 'Queenie' in its home town, this 63 seater had an English Electric body and was one of only five Q type trolleybuses built, of which only two operated in Britain. Southend had the other example, and the remainder operated in Sydney, Australia. The layout of this vehicle was ahead of its time, with a front entrance beside the driver. The high seating capacity proved its worth in wartime South Shields and it lasted in service until the end of 1951. This view shows the vehicle in operation after the war at Marsden Grotto. The limited front destination display is evident and in this instance it is simply showing 'Coast Road'.
(DJ Little coll.)

SEATING PLAN OF UPPER SALOON FOR 33 PASSENGERS

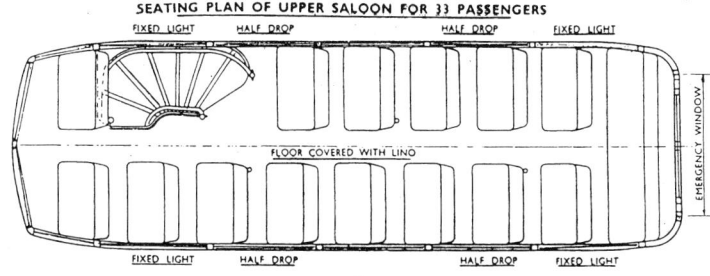

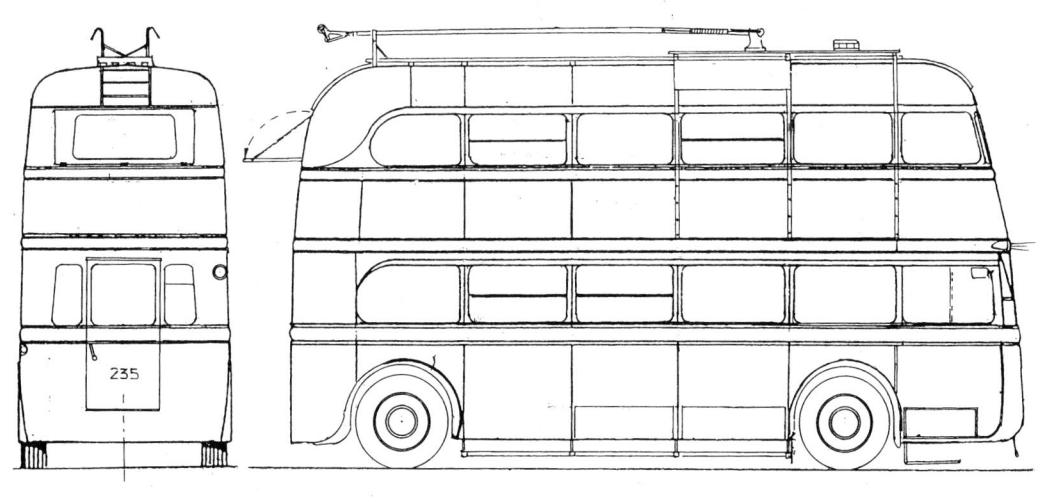

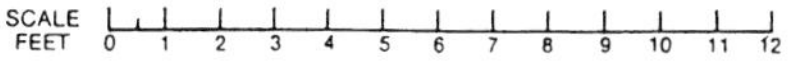

SEATING PLAN OF LOWER SALOON FOR 30 PASSENGERS

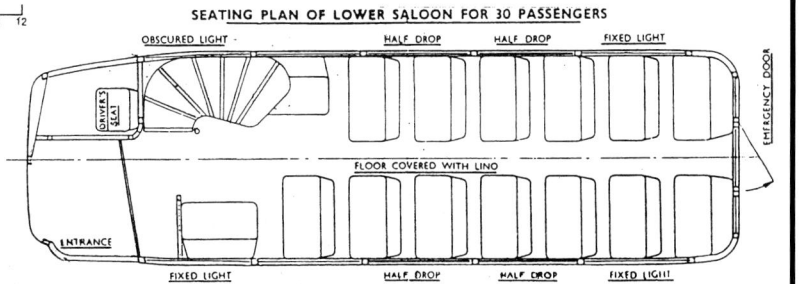

AVAILABLE FROM :- TERRY RUSSELL,
"CHACESIDE", ST. LEONARDS PARK,
HORSHAM, W. SUSSEX. RH13 6EG.

SEND ½ FIRST CLASS STAMPS
FOR COMPLETE LIST OF
PUBLIC TRANSPORT DRAWINGS.

SCALE FEET 0 1 2 3 4 5 6 7 8 9 10 11 12

SOUTH SHIELDS CORPORATION
D/DECK 2 AXLE TROLLEYBUS

Chassis: AEC 761T
Body: English Electric. 1933.
Fleet No. 235. (ex Bradford)
Scale: 4 mm / 1 foot.

DRAWING No. TB68

104   236 (LJ7704)

This vehicle was another unique British trolleybus and a strange sight in South Shields. Acquired from Bournemouth Corporation in 1942, it had a Thorneycroft chassis and a Brush centre-entrance single-deck body seating 32. Built in 1933 as a demonstrator for Thorneycroft and registered CG 4313, it was bought by Bournemouth later that year as part of its original experimental fleet and re-registered. At South Shields it was put to work, initially in Bournemouth livery but with a blue band below the windows, on a short-lived service between Pier Head and the Market Place. In September 1942 it was employed on the new service between Tyne Dock and Horsley Hill, where its seating capacity was woefully inadequate. After the war it operated on the Coast Road service until April 1950 when it was withdrawn, surviving for some years as a static caravan at the Pier Head amusement park. It is seen here at the depot gates in the late 1940s in full South Shields livery. Note the entrance arrangement with a sliding door. (South Tyneside Libraries)

105   237 to 239 (KW 6658, KW 9459, KY 1360)

The continued desperate search for additional vehicles resulted in the purchase in 1945 of this trio of English Electric six-wheel trolleybuses from Bradford Corporation. These trolleybuses dated from 1930, 1931 and 1932 respectively and were from an era when trolleybuses were built resembling trams rather than buses. All these 56 seat vehicles had a different frontal styling. 237 had a straight upper deck front, 238 a rounded one and 239, having been a former demonstration vehicle for its maker, had a sloping panel from the cab edge to the upper deck windows. The former Bradford fleet numbers were 582, 590 and 596. Driving these vehicles was particularly awkward as they had obsolete control equipment and for this reason they were used on the relatively straight Prince Edward Road service to Fremantle Road, and never beyond the Marsden Inn. In any case, the greater height of these vehicles would probably have prevented them passing under the Redwell Lane bridge. They were never painted in South Shields livery retaining their blue Bradford livery (darker blue in the case of 237). The availability of new trolleybuses after the war enabled these vehicles to be withdrawn as soon as possible, 237 in 1946 and the other two in 1947. The photograph shows the vehicle that eventually became 239, when brand new in the green and cream livery of English Electric. (JS King collection)

106   240 to 245 (CU 4601 to 4606)

The first post-war trolleybuses, delivered at the end of 1946, were these six Karrier W4s with Roe utility bodywork. They introduced a simplified version of the livery, without the primrose waistbands. There was no lining-out. Another innovation was the use of carbon-skid trolley heads. During their life some of the vehicles received slider, rather than half drop windows. The first withdrawal came suddenly in November 1962 when 245 overturned at the Marsden Inn (see photograph 115), but 243 and 244 survived until the very end of operation. 245 is seen at the Pier Head in August 1952, Note the lack of exterior advertisements on the vehicle – these were not introduced until a year later. (JH Meredith)

KARRIER "E4"
FOUR-WHEEL TROLLEYBUS CHASSIS

KARRIER TROLLEYBUSES

**107   246 to 248
(CU 4716 to 4718)**

Delivered in the first week of 1947, this trio of Karrier W4 trolleybuses carried a new style of Northern Coachbuilders 56 seat composite bodywork which was built locally in Newcastle. The design was also used on trolleybuses supplied to Newcastle, Maidstone, and Bradford. 246 was withdrawn late in 1962, the remaining two being taken out of stock the following year. 246 is seen in the Market Place in the late 1940s in original condition. Note the lack of a route number display. In the right background is the Tram Hotel, referred to in the caption to photograph 59.
(South Tyneside Libraries)

108   249, 250 (CU 4719, 4720)

Entering service at the same time as the previously described Northern Coachbuilders bodied vehicles, these Karrier W4 trolleybuses reverted to the utility design of Roe bodywork previously used on fleet nos 240 to 245. The only obvious difference was the provision of opening ventilators at the top of the upper deck front windows and sliding, rather than half-drop side windows. Both these vehicles ran until 1963. 250 is seen at the Market Place on 16th April 1952. (R Marshall)

109 251 to 270 (CU 4873 to 4877, 4943 to 4947, 5100 to 5105, 5279 to 5282)

This batch of twenty vehicles, delivered in 1947/8 (251 to 260) and 1950 (261 to 270) completed the new post-war trolleybus fleet. They were broadly similar to nos 246, 247 and 248 delivered earlier in 1947 with Karrier chassis and Northern Coachbuilders 56 seat bodywork but were the first vehicles to be delivered with the ability to display a route number. The 1950 delivery had the updated F4 type chassis and carried triangular Sunbeam badges instead of Karrier. Sunbeam had by then ceased to use the alternative Karrier name. Nevertheless, all these vehicles were referred to in South Shields as 'Karriers'. The 1950 vehicles also had less beading around the bodywork and opening vents to the upper deck front windows. All twenty survived into the last months of the system, the first withdrawal being 261 in August 1963. 260 was the last trolleybus to operate in service. 262 is seen here when newly into service at the Market Place on 24th June 1950. (R Marshall)

110 236 to 239 (GNY 301, 302, FTG 234, 235)

The need to replace more of the older pre-war Karrier trolleybuses led to the purchase from Pontypridd Urban District Council of these second hand vehicles in 1957. These had Karrier W4 chassis built in 1945 (238/9) and 1946 (236/7) with Park Royal utility bodies. They formed part of the eight vehicle Pontypridd trolleybus fleet, all of which were sold in January 1957 when the one-route system closed. The remaining four vehicles were shared equally by the Doncaster and Walsall trolleybus systems. Alterations for service in South Shields included a revised destination layout including the addition of a small destination display above the platform. Although the lower saloon seats were provided with cushions, the original upstairs wooden seats were retained. 236 and 239 had rebuilt front upper deck windows set in rubber. All these vehicles were withdrawn in 1963. The photograph shows 237 in Mile End Road shortly after entering service.
(RF Mack / Trolleybus Museum Company)

111   **201 to 203, 205 to 209 (BDJ 74 to 81)**

Eight second hand trolleybuses joined the fleet in 1958, again to allow more pre-war Karriers to be withdrawn. These came from St Helens Corporation, whose trolleybus system closed on 1st July 1958. They formed half of a batch of 16 vehicles delivered to St Helens in 1950. South Shields took those with Sunbeam F4 chassis, whilst Bradford Corporation bought the remainder which had British United Traction chassis, a type that never ran in South Shields. The bodywork, which was eight feet wide, was all-metal and constructed by East Lancashire Coachbuilders at their Bridlington factory. Alterations carried out by South Shields before entry into service included a revised front destination aperture and a new rear upper deck emergency door. These vehicles had a relatively short life in the town, none of them surviving to the very end of the system. This is 205, formerly numbered 377 in the St Helens fleet, and is seen at Pier Head in 1959 advertising a locally brewed ale. Note that this vehicle is not carrying the bamboo pole above the lower saloon windows as was normal South Shields practice. St Helens used the more conventional underfloor storage tube for this item. (JS King)

ON LOAN

112   In early 1943, the Corporation authorised the Transport Department to hire three Bournemouth trolleybuses for a period of three months to assist the overworked fleet. These vehicles were to Bournemouth's standard design with Sunbeam MS2 six-wheel chassis and Park Royal 56 seat bodies with rear entrance, front exit doors and two staircases. They were the first six-wheel trolleybuses to run on the South Shields system. Their Bournemouth fleet numbers were, 78, 79 and 123 (AEL 406, 407, ALJ 997). Previously in the war, they had operated at London and Newcastle. Arriving in February and March 1943, they ran almost exclusively on the Prince Edward Road service to Fremantle Road, together with Daimler 234. All these vehicles left South Shields at the end of May 1943, nos 78 and 79 then running in Walsall, and all three went on later to operate at Llanelly in South Wales before returning to their home town in mid-1945. These distinctive vehicles in their yellow livery were known as 'Newcastle buses', despite bearing lettering and notices of their true origin. This rather imperfect view is the only known photograph of a Bournemouth vehicle running in South Shields, and shows 123 loading for Prince Edward Road at the Market Place in April 1943. (South Tyneside Libraries)

ON SHOW

113   Decorated trolleybuses were often used to celebrate local and national happenings. For National Savings Week in 1949, Karrier 223 was decorated and illuminated to tour the routes. (South Tyneside Libraries)

114   In May 1953, Karrier 231 (with replacement utility body) was extensively decorated for the Coronation, and it operated a public service on a special schedule during the celebrations. The vehicle is depicted at the Pier Head end of Sea Road, using the alternative turn back wiring for trolleybuses turning at Pier Head, almost on the sea front. This wiring provision was dismantled sometime in the late 1950s. (Newcastle Chronicle and Journal)

ON ITS SIDE

115 This unhappy event occurred on 24th November 1962, when utility 245 hit a traction pole and overturned in Marsden Lane near the Marsden Inn. The view shows the scene immediately after the accident, with the overhead hanging very low above the overturned vehicle. 245 was so badly damaged that it never ran again.
(South Tyneside Libraries)

FINALE

116 During the early months of 1964, the trolleybus system virtually faded away as more and more new motorbuses became available for service. By April only 12 vehicles remained, working on routes 1, 2, 3 and 4, inter-working with the new motorbuses. During the last weeks of service, 269 is seen at the Market Place, in approximately the same position as trolleybus 203 in photograph 101. It is possibly operating a peak-hour extra working and is showing 'Tyne Dock via Commercial Road'. (RDH Symons)

117 The last day was 29th April and that night, 260 performed the final journey from Pier Head to Stanhope Road. Following this, the trolleybuses were banished to the back of the depot awaiting sale to a scrap merchant. 263 is seen at the lower depot having made its last journey in public service.(RDH Symons)

POSTSCRIPT

118 One of the last Karrier E4 vehicles to survive in service was 204, which was withdrawn in 1963. It was acquired by the Reading Transport Society and eventually found a permanent home at the Sandtoft Trolleybus Museum near Doncaster. It is seen here in the early 1950s in the Market Place. Note the Manchester style streamlined livery on the motorbuses, a short-lived feature not applied to the trolleybuses. (C Carter)

←——— 119 One of the first trolleybuses to be privately preserved, 204 spent 40 years after 1963 in a gradual state of decay, awaiting restoration to full working order. It is seen here during this period, in "as withdrawn" condition. (J Fozard)

120   204 was restored to full working order, and launched back into service at the Sandtoft Trolleybus Museum in May 2005. It is seen here in its restored state in 2006. (Author)

MP Middleton Press

EVOLVING THE ULTIMATE RAIL ENCYCLOPEDIA

Easebourne Lane, Midhurst, West Sussex.
GU29 9AZ Tel:01730 813169

www.middletonpress.co.uk email:info@middletonpress.co.uk

A-0 906520 B-1 873793 C-1 901706 D-1 904474

OOP Out of print at time of printing - Please check availability BROCHURE AVAILABLE SHOWING NEW TITLES

A
Abergavenny to Merthyr C 91 8
Abertillery and Ebbw Vale Lines D 84 5
Aldgate & Stepney Tramways B 70 1
Allhallows - Branch Line to A 62 8
Alton - Branch Lines to A 11 6
Andover to Southampton A 82 6
Ascot - Branch Lines around A 64 2
Ashburton - Branch Line to B 95 4
Ashford - Steam to Eurostar B 67 1
Ashford to Dover A 48 2
Austrian Narrow Gauge D 04 3
Avonmouth - BL around D 42 5
Aylesbury to Rugby D 91 3
B
Baker Street to Uxbridge D 90 6
Banbury to Birmingham D 27 2
Barking to Southend C 80 2
Barnet & Finchley Tramways B 93 0
Barry - Branch Lines around D 50 0
Basingstoke to Salisbury A 89 5
Bath Green Park to Bristol C 36 9
Bath to Evercreech Junction A 60 4
Bath Tramways B 86 2
Battle over Portsmouth 1940 A 29 1
Battle over Sussex 1940 A 79 6
Bedford to Wellingborough D 31 9
Betwixt Petersfield & Midhurst A 94 9
Bletchley to Cambridge D 94 4
Bletchley to Rugby E 07 9
Blitz over Sussex 1941-42 B 35 0
Bodmin - Branch Lines around B 83 1
Bognor at War 1939-45 B 59 6
Bombers over Sussex 1943-45 B 51 0
Bournemouth & Poole Trys B 47 3
Bournemouth to Evercreech Jn A 46 8
Bournemouth to Weymouth A 57 4
Bournemouth Trolleybuses C 10 9
Bradford Trolleybuses D 19 7
Brecon to Neath D 43 2
Brecon to Newport D 16 6
Brecon to Newtown E 06 2
Brickmaking in Sussex B 19 0
Brightons Tramways B 02 2 OOP
Brighton to Eastbourne A 16 1
Brighton to Worthing A 03 1
Brighton Trolleybuses D 34 0
Bristols Tramways B 57 2
Bristol to Taunton D 03 6
Bromley South to Rochester B 23 7
Bromsgrove to Birmingham D 87 6
Bromsgrove to Gloucester D 73 9
Brunel - A railtour of his achievements D 74 6
Bude - Branch Line to B 29 9
Burnham to Evercreech Jn A 68 0
Burton & Ashby Tramways C 51 2
C
Camberwell & West Norwood Tys B 22 0
Cambridge to Ely D 55 5
Canterbury - Branch Lines around B 58 9
Cardiff Trolleybuses D 64 7
Caterham & Tattenham Corner B 25 1
Changing Midhurst C 15 4
Chard and Yeovil - BLs around C 30 7
Charing Cross to Dartford A 75 8
Charing Cross to Orpington A 96 3
Cheddar - Branch Line to B 90 9
Cheltenham to Andover C 43 7
Cheltenham to Redditch D 81 4
Chesterfield Tramways D 37 1
Chesterfield Trolleybuses D 51 7
Chester Tramways E 04 8
Chichester to Portsmouth A 14 7
Clapham & Streatham Trams B 97 8
Clapham Junction - 50 yrs C 06 2 OOP
Clapham Junction to Beckenham Jn B 36 7
Clevedon & Portishead - BLs to D 18 0
Collectors Trains, Trolleys & Trams D 29 6
Colonel Stephens D62 3
Cornwall Narrow Gauge D 56 2
Cowdray & Easebourne D 96 8
Crawley to Littlehampton A 34 5
Cromer - Branch Lines around C 26 6
Croydons Tramways B 42 8
Croydons Trolleybuses B 73 2 OOP
Croydon to East Grinstead B 48 0
Crystal Palace (HL) & Catford Loop A 87 1
D
Darlington to Newcastle D 98 2
Darlington Trolleybuses D 33 3
Dartford to Sittingbourne B 34 3
Derby Tramways D 17 3
Derby Trolleybuses C 72 7
Derwent Valley - Branch Line to the D 06 7
Devon Narrow Gauge E 09 3
Didcot to Banbury D 02 9
Didcot to Swindon C 84 0
Didcot to Winchester C 13 0
Dorset & Somerset Narrow Gauge D 76 0
Douglas to Peel C 88 8
Douglas to Port Erin C 55 0
Douglas to Ramsey D 39 5
Dovers Tramways B 24 4
Dover to Ramsgate A 78 9
E
Ealing to Slough C 42 0
Eastbourne to Hastings A 27 7 OOP
East Cornwall Mineral Railways D 22 7
East Croydon to Three Bridges A 53 6
East Grinstead - Branch Lines to A 07 9
East Ham & West Ham Tramways B 52 7
East Kent Light Railway A 61 1 OOP
East London - Branch Lines of C 44 4
East London Line B 80 0
East Ridings Secret Resistance D 21 0
Edgware & Willesden Tramways C 18 5
Effingham Junction - BLs around A 74 1
Eltham & Woolwich Tramways B 74 9 OOP
Ely to Kings Lynn C 53 6
Ely to Norwich C 90 1
Embankment & Waterloo Tramways B 41 1
Enfield & Wood Green Trys C 03 1 OOP
Enfield Town & Palace Gates - BL to D 32 6
Epsom to Horsham A 30 7
Euston to Harrow & Wealdstone C 89 5
Exeter & Taunton Tramways B 32 9
Exeter to Barnstaple B 15 2
Exeter to Newton Abbot C 49 9
Exeter to Tavistock B 69 5
Exmouth - Branch Lines to B 00 8
F
Fairford - Branch Line to A 52 9
Falmouth, Helston & St. Ives - BL to C 74 1
Fareham to Salisbury A 67 3
Faversham to Dover B 05 3
Felixstowe & Aldeburgh - BL to D 20 3
Fenchurch Street to Barking C 20 8
Festiniog - 50 yrs of enterprise C 83 3
Festiniog 1946-55 E 01 7 - PUB 21 APRIL
Festiniog in the Fifties B 68 8
Festiniog in the Sixties B 91 6
Finsbury Park to Alexandra Palace C 02 4
Frome to Bristol B 77 0
Fulwell - Trams, Trolleys & Buses D 11 1
G
Gloucester to Bristol D 35 7
Gloucester to Cardiff D 66 1
Gosport & Horndean Trys B 92 3
Gosport - Branch Lines around A 36 9
Great Yarmouth Tramways D 13 5
Greece Narrow Gauge D 72 2
Greenwich & Dartford Tramways B 14 5 OOP
Grimsby & Cleethorpes Trolleybuses D 86 9
Guildford to Redhill A 63 5 OOP
H
Hammersmith & Hounslow Trys C 33 8
Hampshire Narrow Gauge D 36 4
Hampshire Waterways A 84 0 OOP
Hampstead & Highgate Tramways B 53 4
Harrow to Watford D 14 2
Hastings to Ashford A 37 6
Hastings Tramways B 18 3
Hastings Trolleybuses B 81 7 OOP
Hawkhurst - Branch Line to A 66 6
Hay-on-Wye - Branch Lines around D 92 0
Hayling - Branch Line to A 12 3
Haywards Heath to Seaford A 28 4
Hemel Hempstead - Branch Lines to D 88 3
Henley, Windsor & Marlow - BL to C77 2
Hereford to Newport D 54 8
Hexham to Carlisle D 75 3
Hitchin to Peterborough D 07 4
Holborn & Finsbury Tramways B 79 4
Holborn Viaduct to Lewisham A 81 9
Horsham - Branch Lines to A 02 4
Huddersfield Tramways D 95 1
Huddersfield Trolleybuses C 92 5
Hull Tramways D60 9
Hull Trolleybuses D 24 1
Huntingdon - Branch Lines around A 93 2
I
Ilford & Barking Tramways B 61 9
Ilford to Shenfield C 97 0
Ilfracombe - Branch Line to B 21 3
Ilkeston & Glossop Tramways D 40 1
Industrial Rlys of the South East A 09 3
Ipswich to Saxmundham C 41 3
Ipswich Trolleybuses D 59 3
Isle of Wight Lines - 50 yrs C 12 3
K
Keighley Tramways & Trolleybuses D 83 8
Kent & East Sussex Waterways A 72 X
Kent Narrow Gauge C 45 1
Kent Seaways - Hoys to Hovercraft D 79 1
Kidderminster to Shrewsbury E10 9
Kingsbridge - Branch Line to C 98 7
Kingston & Hounslow Loops A 83 3 OOP
Kingston & Wimbledon Tramways B 56 5
Kingswear - Branch Line to C 17 8
L
Lambourn - Branch Line to C 70 3
Launceston & Princetown - BL to C 19 2
Lewisham & Catford Tramways B 26 8 OOP
Lewisham to Dartford A 92 5
Lines around Wimbledon B 75 6
Liverpool Street to Chingford D 01 2
Liverpool Street to Ilford C 34 5
Liverpool Tramways - Eastern C 04 8
Liverpool Tramways - Northern C 46 8
Liverpool Tramways - Southern C 23 9
London Bridge to Addiscombe B 20 6
London Bridge to East Croydon A 58 1
London Chatham & Dover Railway A 88 8
London Termini - Past and Proposed D 00 5
London to Portsmouth Waterways B 43 5
Longmoor - Branch Lines to A 41 3
Looe - Branch Line to C 22 2
Lyme Regis - Branch Line to A 45 1
Lynton - Branch Line to B 04 6
M
Maidstone & Chatham Tramways B 40 4
Maidstone Trolleybuses C 00 0 OOP
March - Branch Lines around B 09 1
Margate & Ramsgate Tramways C 52 9
Marylebone to Rickmansworth D49 4
Melton Constable to Yarmouth Beach E 03 1
Midhurst - Branch Lines around A 49 9
Midhurst - Branch Lines to A 01 7 OOP
Military Defence of West Sussex A 23 9
Military Signals, South Coast C 54 3
Minehead - Branch Line to A 80 2
Mitcham Junction Lines B 01 5
Mitchell & company C 59 8
Monmouthshire Eastern Valleys D 71 5
Moreton-in-Marsh to Worcester D 26 5
Moretonhampstead - BL to C 27 7
Mountain Ash to Neath D 80 7
N
Newbury to Westbury C 66 6
Newcastle to Hexham D 69 2
Newcastle Trolleybuses D 78 4
Newport (IOW) - Branch Lines to A 26 0
Newquay - Branch Lines to C 71 0
Newton Abbot to Plymouth C 60 4
Northern France Narrow Gauge C 75 8
North East German Narrow Gauge D 44 9
North Kent Tramways B 44 2
North London Line B 94 7
North Woolwich - BLs around C 65 9
Norwich Tramways C 40 6
Nottinghamshire & Derbyshire T/B D 63 0
Nottinghamshire & Derbyshire T/W D 53 1
O
Ongar - Branch Lines to E 05 5
Orpington to Tonbridge B 03 9 OOP
Oxford to Bletchley D57 9
Oxford to Moreton-in-Marsh D 15 9
P
Paddington to Ealing C 37 6
Paddington to Princes Risborough C 81 9
Padstow - Branch Line to B 54 1
Plymouth - BLs around B 98 5
Plymouth to St. Austell C 63 5
Pontypool to Mountain Ash D 65 4
Porthmadog 1954-94 - BL around B 31 2
Porthmadog to Blaenau B 50 3 OOP
Portmadoc 1923-46 - BL around B 13 8
Portsmouths Tramways B 72 5
Portsmouth to Southampton A 31 4
Portsmouth Trolleybuses C 73 4
Potters Bar to Cambridge D 70 8
Princes Risborough - Branch Lines to D 05 0
Princes Risborough to Banbury C 85 7
R
Railways to Victory C 16 1 OOP
Reading to Basingstoke B 27 5
Reading to Didcot C 79 6
Reading to Guildford A 47 5 OOP
Reading Tramways B 87 9
Reading Trolleybuses C 05 5
Redhill to Ashford A 73 4
Return to Blaenau 1970-82 C 64 2
Rickmansworth to Aylesbury D 61 6
Roman Roads of Hampshire D 67 8
Roman Roads of Kent E 02 4
Roman Roads of Surrey C 61 1
Roman Roads of Sussex C 48 2
Romneyrail C 32 1
Ryde to Ventnor A 19 2
S
Salisbury to Westbury B 39 8
Salisbury to Yeovil B 06 0 OOP
Saxmundham to Yarmouth C 69 7
Saxony Narrow Gauge D 47 0
Seaton & Eastbourne Tramways B 76 3 OOP
Seaton & Sidmouth - Branch Lines to A 95 6
Secret Sussex Resistance B 82 4
SECR Centenary album C 11 6
Selsey - Branch Line to A 04 8
Sheerness - Branch Lines around B 16 9
Shepherds Bush to Uxbridge T/Ws C 28 4
Shrewsbury - Branch Line to A 86 4
Sierra Leone Narrow Gauge D 28 9
Sirhowy Valley Line E 12 3
Sittingbourne to Ramsgate A 90 1
Slough to Newbury C 56 7
Solent - Creeks, Crafts & Cargoes D 52 4
Southamptons Tramways B 33 6
Southampton to Bournemouth A 42 0
Southend-on-Sea Tramways B 28 2
Southern France Narrow Gauge C 47 5
Southwark & Deptford Tramways B 38 1
Southwold - Branch Line to A 15 4
South Eastern & Chatham Railways C 08 6
South London Line B 46 6
South London Tramways 1903-33 D 10 4
South London Tramways 1933-52 D 89 0
South Shields Trolleybuses E 11 6
St. Albans to Bedford D 08 1
St. Austell to Penzance C 67 3
St. Pancras to Barking D 68 5
St. Pancras to St. Albans C 78 9
Stamford Hill Tramways B 85 5
Steaming through Cornwall B 30 5 OOP
Steaming through Kent A 13 0 OOP
Steaming through the Isle of Wight A 56 7
Steaming through West Hants A 69 7
Stratford upon avon to Birmingham D 77 7
Stratford upon Avon to Cheltenham C 25 3
Strood to Paddock Wood B 12 1 OOP
Surrey Home Guard C 57 4
Surrey Narrow Gauge C 87 1
Surrey Waterways A 51 2 OOP
Sussex Home Guard C 24 6
Sussex Narrow Gauge C 68 0
Sussex Shipping Sail, Steam & Motor D 23 4 OOP
Swanley to Ashford B 45 9
Swindon to Bristol C 96 3
Swindon to Gloucester D46 3
Swindon to Newport D 30 2
Swiss Narrow Gauge C 94 9
T
Talyllyn - 50 years C 39 0
Taunton to Barnstaple B 60 2
Taunton to Exeter C 82 6
Tavistock to Plymouth B 88 6
Tees-side Trolleybuses D 58 6
Tenterden - Branch Line to A 21 5
Thanets Tramways B 11 4 OOP
Three Bridges to Brighton A 35 2
Tilbury Loop C 86 4
Tiverton - Branch Lines around C 62 8
Tivetshall to Beccles D 41 8
Tonbridge to Hastings A 44 4
Torrington - Branch Lines to B 37 4
Tunbridge Wells - Branch Lines to A 32 1
Twickenham & Kingston Trys C 35 2
Two-Foot Gauge Survivors C 21 5 OOP
U
Upwell - Branch Line to B 64 0
V
Victoria & Lambeth Tramways B 49 7
Victoria to Bromley South A 98 7
Victoria to East Croydon A 40 6 OOP
Vivarais C 31 4 OOP
Vivarais Revisited E 08 6
W
Walthamstow & Leyton Tramways B 65 7
Waltham Cross & Edmonton Trys C 07 9
Wandsworth & Battersea Tramways B 63 3
Wantage - Branch Line to D 25 8
Wareham to Swanage - 50 yrs D 09 8
War on the Line A 10 9
War on the Line VIDEO + 88 0
Waterloo to Windsor A 54 3
Waterloo to Woking A 38 3
Watford to Leighton Buzzard D 45 6
Wenford Bridge to Fowey C 09 3
Westbury to Bath B 55 8
Westbury to Taunton C 76 5
West Cornwall Mineral Railways D 48 7
West Croydon to Epsom B 08 4
West German Narrow Gauge D 93 7
West London - Branch Lines of C 50 5
West London Line B 84 8
West Sussex Waterways A 24 6 OOP
West Wiltshire - Branch Lines of D 12 8
Weymouth - Branch Lines around A 65 9
Willesden Junction to Richmond B 71 8
Wimbledon to Beckenham C 58 1
Wimbledon to Epsom B 62 6
Wimborne - Branch Lines around A 97 0
Wisbech - Branch Lines around C 01 7
Wisbech 1800-1901 C 93 2
Woking to Alton A 59 8
Woking to Portsmouth A 25 3
Woking to Southampton A 55 0
Wolverhampton Trolleybuses D 85 2
Woolwich & Dartford Trolleys B 66 4
Worcester to Birmingham D 97 5
Worcester to Hereford D 38 8
Worthing to Chichester A 06 2
Y
Yeovil - 50 yrs change C 38 3
Yeovil to Dorchester A 76 5 OOP
Yeovil to Exeter A 91 8
York Tramways & Trolleybuses D 82 1

Index

Alternating current (AC) 7, 22, 27
Asymmetric Brake Control (ABC Braking) 45, 46
'Aviation' plugs and sockets 104, 106, 109

Backscene 113, 129
Ballast 14-17, 121, 129
Baseboards 10ff, 100-03
    framing and bracing 11, 100, 102
    materials 10
    trestles and legs 11-12, 101-02, 103, 104
Bits and bytes, explanation of 50-52
Bluetooth control 26
'Bread board' project board 72
Bridges 110-11, 112, 114-15, 117
Buildings
    external detailing 30-31
    internal detailing and lighting 28-29, 55-56
'Bus' wires 18, 19; DCC 46-47, 106
    twin-bus system 47-48

Cab control 23
Cable ducting, concrete 81
Capacitor Discharge Unit (CDU) 35, 36-37, 66, 72
Capacitors 64-67
Carriage lighting 54-55
'Centre-off' switches 23
Configuration Variable (CV) 41, 50, 52
Construction kits 28ff
    downloadable 32
    techniques 30
    tools required 29-30
Control panel 108-09
Controllers 22, 23

Digital Command Control (DCC) 7, 18, 22, 24-26, 27, 36, 38ff, 54, 104, 107, 109-10
    accessory decoders 42-43, 47
    Boosters 45, 46, 47
    circuit breakers 47

'Configuration Variables' (CVs) 41, 50, 52
    decoders 7, 24, 39-41
    filters 48, 49
    locomotives 41
    problems and fixes 48-50
    wi-fi connections 25
    wiring 46, 48
Diodes 67-68
Direct Current (DC) 7, 22-23, 26-27, 35, 62
Double Pole Double Throw (DPDT) switches 23, 35, 45
Dropper wires 18, 19, 21; DCC 46-47, 106

Fencing 76, 117
Fishplates 7
Fogging huts 79

Goods sheds 79
Goods yards, lighting of 77-78
Ground cover 32

Infrared 74; train detector 126
Insulated Rail Joiners (IRJ) 8, 23, 44, 45
Integrated Circuit Dual In Line (IC DIL) socket 36
Integrated Circuits (IC) 70ff
Isopropanol Alcohol (IPA) 16, 97

Light Emitting Diodes (LEDs) 29, 54, 55-56, 67, 68, 73, 74, 77-78, 85, 108, 124
    strips 57, 124
Lighting of layout 18, 19, 29, 56-58, 77, 122-23, 130

Overhead Line Equipment (OLE) 92-97

Peripheral Interface Controller (PIC) circuits 57, 59, 73, 126
Permanent way huts 78-79
Plaster bandage, as scenic base 125, 127, 128
Platforms and canopies 111, 113, 124

Points 8, 13, 33ff, 105
    motors 8, 19, 27, 33
    relays, latching and unlatching 35, 36, 37, 42
    rodding 33, 80-81
    servos 34, 35, 105, 108
    'stud and probe' 35
    switches 34
    wire-in-tube 33
Printed Circuit Boards (PCB) 36
Pulse Width Modulation (PWM) control 22-23
PVA glue, use of 16-17, 30, 32, 60, 104

Rail cleaning 97-98
Resistors 62-64
Reverse Loop Module (RLM) 43-45

Scales 8
Signal boxes 79-80, 120
Signalling, colour light 84, 85-87, 123, 126
    ground signals 87-88
    junction route indicator ('feather' and 'theatre') 85-86
    semaphore 82-84

Single Pole Double Throw (SPDT) switches 23, 34, 35
Soldering and soldering irons 19, 20-21
Solenoids 33, 35, 36
Static grass 32, 60-61
'Suitcase' connectors 20

Telegraph poles 75-77
Third rail electrification 89-92
Toggle switches 34
Track 13ff, 104, 105
    cork underlay 14
    cross-baseboard connections 104-05
    flexible 13-14
    foam trackbed 15
    painting 15
Transistors 68-69

Voltage regulator circuits 70-71

Weathering 28
Wire, choice of 18-19
    connectors 20, 47, 106